Containment and Reciprocity

"Based on Douglas' doctoral work this book is the outcome of an exciting and stimulating project to bring together the psychoanalytic concept of containment and the concept of reciprocity from child development research to form a single clinical approach to working with young children and their families and to individual work with older children. It is a readable and accessible book, which is of interest to all involved in such work. Its detailed exploration of both concepts and their interrelationship makes it a satisfying read for those who would like to further and enrich their clinical work and theoretical understanding by integrating concepts from disciplines other than their own."

Sue Coulson, Head of Child and Adolescent Psychotherapy
Islington PCT, Visiting Teacher, Tavistock Clinic

"A timely piece of writing. Hazel Douglas has rigorously explored the theories of containment and reciprocity and their uses in working with children. By her careful tracking of these two themes, in both psychoanalysis and child development research, she has begun to remove the imagined demarcation lines between these two areas of discipline. This book is very enabling and will be of great use to many working in the field of child mental health."

Nina Harris, Consultant Child and Adolescent Psychotherapist

Containment and Reciprocity shows how the psychoanalytic concept of containment and the child development concept of reciprocity can be used together to inform clinical work with young children and their families. Using extracts of mother/child and therapist/child interactions, Hazel Douglas explores, for the first time, the relationship between these concepts, and shows how they underpin the quality of an attachment.

Using clinical examples from the author's own psychoanalytic work with very young children as well as her recent research, the book explores these two concepts with important implications for psychotherapeutic technique. *Containment and Reciprocity* will make valuable reading for all those working in the field of infant mental health.

Hazel Douglas trained first as a clinical psychologist and then as a child psychotherapist. She has always had an interest in early intervention and prevention. She began working with adults but she is now working with infant mental health. She leads the development of the Solihull Approach, an integrated method of working with children and their families.

Containment and Reciprocity

Integrating psychoanalytic theory and child development research for work with children

Hazel Douglas

Routledge
Taylor & Francis Group

LONDON AND NEW YORK

First published 2007 by Routledge
27 Church Road, Hove, East Sussex BN3 2FA

Simultaneously published in the USA and Canada
by Routledge
270 Madison Avenue, New York, NY 10016

Routledge is an imprint of the Taylor & Francis Group, an informa business

Typeset in Times by Garfield Morgan, Swansea, West Glamorgan
Printed and bound in Great Britain by TJ International Ltd, Padstow,
Cornwall
Paperback cover design by Design Deluxe Ltd

This publication has been produced with paper manufactured to strict
environmental standards and with pulp derived from sustainable
forests.

British Library Cataloguing in Publication Data
A catalogue record for this book is available from the British Library

Library of Congress Cataloging in Publication Data
Douglas, Hazel, 1956–
    Containment and reciprocity : integrating psychoanalytic theory and
child development research for work with children / Hazel Douglas.
        p. ; cm.
    Includes bibliographical references and index.
    ISBN-13: 978-0-415-39697-4 (hardback)
    ISBN-10: 0-415-39697-2 (hardback)
    ISBN-13: 978-0-415-39698-1 (pbk.)
    ISBN-10: 0-415-39698-0 (pbk.)
1. Child psychotherapy. 2. Psychotherapist and patient. I. Title.
    [DNLM: 1. Psychoanalytic Therapy–methods. 2. Behavior
Therapy–methods. 3. Child, Preschool. 4. Infant. 5. Parent-Child
Relations. 6. Professional-Patient Relations. WS 350.5 D734c 2007]
    RJ499.D66 2007
    618.92'8914–dc22
                                                            2006035855
ISBN: 978-0-415-39697-4 (hbk)
ISBN: 978-0-415-39698-1 (pbk)

For my parents, Geoffrey and Hannalore

Contents

Foreword

One of the saddest phrases in our vocabulary is 'too late'. At its most poignant, it refers to the discovery, in adult life, of the irretrievable opportunities that the early environment failed to provide. On rare occasions, such missed opportunities are the outcome of deliberate parental malice. But to think only in such terms is misleading. Far more commonly, parents struggle painfully in the face of difficulties. Like the infant, they can be left feeling robbed of all the promise that a good beginning can hold. It is sobering to discover that the infant's earliest experiences will define her basic expectations from the world for many years to come, as well as crucial aspects of her mental resilience and ability to relate and be happy.

Parenting a newborn is a delicate task, but infants can survive a great deal of everyday anxiety and discomfort, provided that the overall family experience is good enough. On the positive side, infancy also provides a unique opportunity to offer support to the family at a crucial time. How encouraging, therefore, that an increasing number of researchers and clinicians continue to turn their attention to the study and treatment of infants and their parents. How encouraging also, to discover the huge gains made in both research and clinical technique since the 1970s. And of course, discoveries about early life inform the understanding and treatment of older children.

Hazel Douglas is one of the professionals dedicated to this area of work. An experienced child psychotherapist with a background in psychology, Hazel first made a contribution to the growing field of infant and child mental health by setting up a valuable project and establishing its principles in the Solihull Approach. There are numerous excellent projects on infant mental health around the world, many of them rightly proud of the model they have developed. Where Douglas is distinctive is in her way of disseminating essential conceptual tools to frontline workers. And after much study and extensive experience, she has found the most powerful tools in the psycho-analytic concept of 'containment' and the child development research concept of 'reciprocity'.

Douglas discovered that both concepts are highly applicable, and can be understood and used in pragmatic ways by a range of practitioners. This is due to the fact that, while being theoretically sophisticated, they make intuitive sense, and speak to our innate human knowledge of relating. Both concepts offer much that goes beyond deductive treatment models which focus on the modification of behaviour. Yet both, if used well, have the power to alter fundamental relational patterns, and therefore represent the possibility of continuing change.

But Douglas was faced with a difficulty. Professionals were rarely using both concepts to inform their clinical interventions. The concepts come from different though related fields, psychoanalysis and child development. Each field has its own conceptual language, its own approach to discovery and formulation. Professionals were deterred by the thought of drawing on different conceptual frameworks based on different perspectives on mental life. The role of unconscious experience was but one of the issues at stake.

Yet Douglas also saw an important complementarity that helps to group 'containment' and 'reciprocity' as relational in nature, and thus different from approaches that emphasise the role of intellectual cognition over emotions and relating. Having successfully established the Solihull Project, and produced learning materials to disseminate it more broadly, she decided to undertake a theoretical study of both concepts. She embarked on doctoral work with the aim of identifying possibilities of encompassing both concepts in a single clinical approach.

In this book, based on her doctoral research, Douglas explores the theoretical histories and clinical application of 'containment' and 'reciprocity'. Drawing on a wealth of professional literature, she brings together a large body of knowledge in a succinct and lively way. A fascinating picture of infant mental life begins to emerge for the reader, based on research findings from child development studies and enriched by the depth of psychoanalytic understanding. Douglas gradually works her way into the clinical situation, showing how both concepts can be encompassed in a single outlook, aiding the therapist's formulations and technique.

Her work reminds us that therapeutic work with infants, young children and their families must be informed by a complex understanding, yet avoid the artificiality of a theory-driven approach. By thinking in terms of containment and reciprocity, the practitioner can become an aware participant in the family experience prior to drawing conclusions about the required help. This also depends on the willingness to observe many fine-grained details, by drawing out the natural patterns of interaction of the parents with their infant. Of course, Douglas's work has implications for the treatment of older children as well. 'Reciprocity' and 'containment' are equally crucial for the therapy of the individual child. Both concepts remind us that our understanding of other individuals is many-layered, nuanced and finely structured. In helping others, nothing can replace our willingness to work for this level of understanding. Providing it to young patients can never start too early.

Meira Likierman
5 November 2006

Acknowledgements

Many thanks to my parents for their encouragement; to my partner for patience and support; to Sue Coulson, who supervised my work with 'Kylie', for debating the initial ideas with me and allowing me the space to think; to Meira Likierman and Anne Alvarez for their careful thought and time, in the midst of very busy schedules, for reading, correcting and discussing the drafts for my doctorate, which formed the basis of this book; and to my colleagues in Solihull and the Solihull Approach team as we learn together. A special thanks to 'Kylie' and her family.

1 Both/and, not either/or

All over the world, those of us working with very young children and their families are having to perform mental gymnastics, climbing out of our favourite theoretical box in order to integrate concepts from different fields. Working with infants means that we need to work quickly, so that valuable developmental time is not lost. This requires us to try new approaches. In addition, a baby and his family present many facets at the same time: the baby himself, his relationship with his mother, his relationship with his father, his relationship with his parents together, the parents' relationship, each parent's mental health and its relationship to the parents' own previous parenting, the way the family functions, and the way the extended family functions, the presence or not of support in the community. This represents many different theories all at the same time. I am going to take two influential concepts from different areas, describe them and their relationship, and then show how they can inform clinical work when the practitioner is aware of the phenomena which the concepts try to describe. The two concepts are containment (Bion, 1959) from the psychoanalytic world and reciprocity (Brazelton et al., 1974) from the child development research community. These two concepts, together with behaviour management from learning theory, comprise the Solihull Approach, a model of working with infants and their families, which is described elsewhere (Douglas, 2004a). These concepts have proved to be helpful both for professionals (Douglas & Ginty, 2001; Whitehead & Douglas, 2005) and for parents (Douglas & Brennan, 2004; Milford et al., 2006). This book provides the space to explore the concepts in more detail, extending both theory and practice.

Describing and naming the relationship between the two concepts allows the interplay to be seen and used with greater clinical precision. Wittgenstein suggested that naming within language, constructing a name for something, allows it then to be thought about: 'what we cannot speak about we must pass over in silence' (Wittgenstein, 1921/2001: Proposition 7, p. 89). Although both these concepts have names, these names are used mainly within their own discipline, and each is not generally used within the other's field. This means that each community is missing out on using the rich explanatory concept of the other. This situation is exacerbated by the fact that containment as a concept has been created and mainly used in the UK, whereas reciprocity has been described and mainly developed within the USA. By bringing both these concepts to awareness at the same time, it should be possible to extend our understanding of the interrelationship.

In order to examine the concepts in more detail, I will first attempt to define them. The curious situation exists that, although containment is one of the most influential ideas within British psychoanalytic circles, it is not defined in any of the psychoanalytic dictionaries. Nor have its theoretical ramifications been explored in any detail. I will also define reciprocity and, in addition, look at its relationship with the three linked ideas of attunement, intersubjectivity and mutual affect regulation. The concepts of attunement, intersubjectivity and mutual affect regulation have all developed from reciprocity, but there has been little work carried out in describing their subsequent relationship.

I think that containment and reciprocity are fundamental in human society. They are the basic building material of the architecture of human relationships. I think that they are therefore also the mechanisms through which the quality of an attachment is created. I will examine both research and therapeutic interventions to show that both containment and reciprocity are involved in the creation of the quality of an attachment.

It will probably be difficult at times for psychoanalytic psychotherapists and for child developmentalists to read this book, because each will feel at times that I have not done justice to 'their' concept, especially as I shall be looking at each concept from the perspective of the other. Each concept has grown within a particular literature that I shall only be able to present a small proportion of. I therefore apologise in advance for when I have been unable to represent the full richness of the idea, but hope that you will bear with me during the exploration.

Containment and reciprocity: a first look

At this point, I will introduce the concepts by providing a definition the result of my examination of some of the literature on containment and reciprocity. Material will be provided later to show how the following definitions of containment and reciprocity have been arrived at. 'Emotional communication' includes anxiety, fear and terror.

Containment is thought to occur when one person receives and understands the emotional communication of another without being overwhelmed by it and communicates this back to the other person. This process can restore the capacity to think in the other person.

Reciprocity initially describes the sophisticated interactions between a baby and an adult when both are involved in the initiation, regulation and termination of the interaction. Reciprocity applies to the interactions in all relationships.

Both containment and reciprocity are involved in the interrelationship between two people. However, within the mother/baby relationship, the mother is portrayed as much more active in the concept of containment, whereas both mother and baby are portrayed as active within the concept of reciprocity.

The process of reciprocity has been captured by video, through a frame-by-frame analysis (Brazelton et al., 1974). It can be observed directly in the behaviours of the participants. It is both a conscious and unconscious process. Containment tends to be more of an unconscious process, although one can also consciously act to contain another. The process of containment has not yet been studied by analysis of videotape, although it may be possible in the future. Judith Trowell (2003) has suggested that it may be possible to perform a microanalysis of eye movements and other eye-related phenomena to examine containment. There may be other observable concomitants as well, such as other facial responses and body posture. At present, however, containment tends to be inferred from the end result, where the other person quietens/becomes calmer or is able to change their behaviour. Further similarities and differences will be outlined later.

Clinical experience, theory development and the *Zeitgeist*

For me, the idea of using containment and reciprocity, two concepts from disparate fields, has grown in a space defined by three different lines of thought. Britton (1989) suggested that creativity occurs within a thinking space originally occurring in childhood within the Oedipal triangle created by the triangulation between the father, mother and child. Here, the triangulation is provided by the link between the following three lines of thought. The first is clinical experience. The second is from a step in the natural evolution of theory. The third is the prevailing international *Zeitgeist* around work in infant mental health.

Clinical experience is the first contributory factor. Two types of clinical experience influenced my thinking. The first was the process of working to understand my clinical experiences in the therapy room with an individual young child and suspecting that current psycho-analytic theory was not sufficient to explain my experiences. The second was in listening to health visitors discuss their work with infants and their families, and in thinking about my own work with families with very young children.

In my individual clinical work, the therapeutic method that I used was psychoanalytic psychotherapy based on object relations theory. This theory is prevalent in the UK. The essence of object relations theory is that human beings are not simple nuclear selves: we are all in a constant relationship to 'objects' or internal representations of other people or aspects of other people (Hinshelwood, 1991). These internal representations may be based on actual external relationships, but they are also affected by our own inner constructions of them. Although Klein herself emphasised that both internal and external reality were important, there was sometimes a tendency in early psychotherapeutic work with children to minimise the importance of the outside world. Although this was useful in developing the theory, current practice now tends to incorporate a better balance between knowledge of the external reality of the child and working with the internal world of the child in the therapy room.

The method of psychoanalytic psychotherapy based on object relations theory is that the therapist is constantly attempting to understand and interpret the internal world of the child as it becomes manifest in the therapy, both in the relationship with the therapist and with the play material in the room. The ideas around containment and reciprocity in this book first crystallised around the experience of working with this psychotherapeutic method with a little girl whom I shall call Kylie. The initial ideas about these concepts were first discussed in a paper (Douglas, 2002). Kylie was about three and a half years old when we first met for twice-weekly psychoanalytic psycho-therapy for six months, progressing to thrice-weekly therapy for three years. It is typical of this type of therapy that it is possible to gain a glimpse of the child's infantile aspect; that is, there were times in the sessions when it was like working with an infant or very young child, and I began to think about the relationship between the theory of reciprocity from child development research (Brazelton et al., 1974), which had been developed from the observation of mothers with their infants, and the theory of containment. The concept of containment was first suggested by Bion in 1959 in response to a deeper understanding of the counter-transference. This will be expanded upon later.

Kylie was an engaging but very anxious little girl. Internal doors in the house had to be kept shut or she would become extremely anxious if she walked past an open door. She felt compelled to change her clothes six or seven times a day and would wash her hands many times after going to the toilet or if they became dirty. She had other obsessional rituals, which she performed to lessen and control her anxiety, becoming extremely upset if she was prevented from doing so. This was distressing both to her and to her parents.

The background to this was that, before Kylie was born, her sister Mary was seriously injured in a traffic accident when Mary was three years old. Her parents struggled to keep Mary alive, but, although there were times of hope, eventually Mary died seven months later. Kylie was born five months after Mary's death. Kylie's parents were still grieving for Mary when Kylie was born and no doubt were recovering from seven months of physical and emotional strain. Kylie also had a brother, Connor, who was six years older than her.

There was evidence that her parents' ability to provide the containment needed by Kylie was compromised. Her parents were, understandably, often preoccupied with their own distress, making it difficult for them to attend to Kylie's moments of distress. This process is not uncommon in this type of situation and has been documented by Reid (1993). The parents' grief was still very evident four years later.

In the parent sessions, tears were never very far away whenever Mary was mentioned. Although this was very understandable, this contributed to the situation described by Bion (1959), where the child is left with their own terror, overcome with nameless dread, which the child has to try and control or defend against. When parents are grieving in this type of situation, it can be difficult for them to offer all the requisite developmental support. Such preoccupations may interfere with parents' availability to be involved with the surviving infant in a reciprocal relationship. However, in this case, Kylie's parents recognised her plight and sought help for her, arranging their lives around bringing Kylie to therapy three times a week, no small feat within a busy family life.

The inferred result of these external events was that Kylie's inner world was peopled by depressed, dead or unresponsive objects. As the therapy progressed, I became aware that she was often stuck in a very persecuting world, in psychotherapeutic terms, a paranoid-schizoid mode of functioning (Klein, 1946/1988), frightened that she had killed off her sister and her functioning parents and frightened that her aggression would rebound on her as the debilitated objects redirected her projected anger back on her. She would then try to control this vicious circle with external rituals, having few inner containing resources of her own. At other times she would 'disintegrate' within the session, something that was very distressing to behold, the session descending into mess and chaos.

Details of Kylie's clinical material will be considered later in order to identify where the concepts of containment and/or reciprocity were utilised within the reciprocal interaction with Kylie in order to explain the behaviour of the patient and the therapist. Neither by itself seemed adequate. The experience of working with Kylie was pivotal in developing my understanding of both these concepts and led to my questioning of how reciprocity was involved within the practice of psychoanalytic psychotherapy and how the psychoanalytic concept of containment related to the child development concept of reciprocity. This was an example of 'learning by doing' (Kolb, 1985), where the actual experience provided the impetus to integrate mentally different theoretical concepts. This case also represented more than itself. The experience within this case helped to integrate the experience of my own analysis, my learning from my training as a child psychotherapist and experience from my work with other individual cases. It also provided the platform from which to question my understanding of my work with families and health visitors' work with families.

Health visitors are a professional group working within the UK. They are initially trained as nurses and then specialise later as health visitors. Every family within the UK has access to a health visitor. They increasingly try to visit every family antenatally, and then carry out a primary visit when the baby is around ten days old. Some areas provide further visits for every family; others provide further visits for those in need. They also run well-baby clinics, antenatal groups and post-natal groups. In many areas, health visitors are available to the family for the first four years; in some areas, for much longer than this. For many families, health visitors provide the first contact point when difficulties arise between parents and children. As I had trained as both a psychologist and as a child psychotherapist, when I worked with health visitors to think about what concepts might be most useful to them in their work, my experience led me to suggest the use of containment together with the behaviour management that they were already familiar with. However, it soon became apparent that these two concepts together were not enough to illuminate and direct the work with infants and their families. A concept was required that would focus on the active relationship between the parents and child. I knew of Brazelton's concept of reciprocity, and when we applied the understanding from this concept together with containment, the work leapt forward and continues to do so in the form of the Solihull Approach (Douglas, 2004a). Although we use other ideas as well within the clinical situation, the concepts of containment and reciprocity seem to be robust enough to provide the foundation for work with families that enables families to change and in doing so, to solve some of the difficulties that arise.

The evolution of theory is the second influential factor in the genesis of the ideas within this book. Concepts go through a time of defining themselves, usually against other concepts, where the emphasis is on difference, as in the relationship of teenagers with their parents. It may be that theories mature a little like people, in that during adolescence the person moves towards separation and individuation in order to prepare for making a relationship with another. As the concept develops and people become more confident in their application, it becomes more possible to examine interrelationships.

This may be linked to, but not completely comparable with, the philosopher Hegel's dialectic process, which is a very interesting idea. Hegel thought that whenever there was a thesis there was also an opposite antithesis and that eventually a resolution would be formed out of these opposites, which would be the synthesis. The concepts of containment and reciprocity are not exactly opposites, but they are different and can seem to have less of a relationship than opposites (in that opposites are related to each other by the fact that they are opposite). Containment and reciprocity are not entirely antithetical, but they are different enough to require a synthesis. Hegel's view was that ideas evolve within a dynamic tension between them (Magee, 1998). Thus, within this book, a similar process of development may occur of defining the thesis, antithesis and synthesis, that is, by first defining containment and reciprocity and then examining how containment and reciprocity are similar and how they are different, and then how they can both be used in work with young children (the synthesis).

Alan Shuttleworth (1999) has written about the evolution of psychoanalytic theory. He has outlined the development of psychoanalytic thinking, about the causes of 'serious, complex and persistent child mental health disorders' (Shuttleworth, 1999, p. 1), through three phases. He emphasised the use of the term 'phase' rather than 'stage', because all three forms of theory are in use today, although each phase needed its predecessor from which to evolve. The first phase was the early theory of Freud where disorders were thought to arise from conflicting states of desire, especially infantile sexuality and aggression. The second phase was the later theory of Freud and Klein where disorders arose from 'disordered states of identification, understood as internal states' (Shuttleworth, 1999, p. 2). The third phase of theory was developed between 1958 and 1962 by Bion, Bowlby and Winnicott. They postulated that childhood disorders arose from 'damage to the intimate early processes of interaction between a child and her or his parents' (Shuttleworth, 1999, p. 3). Shuttleworth names this as the theory of attachment-holding-containment. This is not to say that each component theory is the same. Differences exist, but there is an overlap between them. Shuttleworth suggests that a fourth phase of development of theory will need to reach beyond psychoanalytic theory so as to integrate theoretical developments from other disciplines. Hopefully, the ideas outlined in this book may contribute to this fourth phase of development, in that I have attempted to define and integrate two different concepts from two different disciplines, one from the psychoanalytic world and one from the child development research world.

The third influence is the current *Zeitgeist* (spirit of the times) within the field of infant mental health, which appears to be a move towards integration. '*Zeitgeist*' is also a term developed by Hegel, one aspect of which is that the development of ideas occurs within a historical context. There are many examples now of individuals arguing that it is important to integrate theories. Douglas and Brennan (2004) pointed out that Scavo (2000), a child psychiatrist working in Italy, thought that psychoanalytic, interactional and behaviourist models converge in working with parents and young children, because of the demands of this particular type of work. It may be that the therapists working with young children and their families are using 'combined theory' in their work because the situation demands interventions at different points in the system all at once. The therapist is faced with a mother, a child, and the interaction between the mother and child, which is further complicated by the relationship between the mother and father, family and grandparents, and the father and child, all at a time when the needs of the child demand rapid change. Scavo described the different emphases of the different theories as follows:

> The psychodynamic model focuses primarily on maternal representations, the behaviourist model focuses primarily on interactive behaviours, and those who observe the meaning of affective

changes from a dynamic point of view, focus on the nature of the relationship. Finally, infant psychoanalysts and developmental psychologists focus on the child's qualities and the developing construction of his /her inner world.

(Scavo, 2000, p. 2)

Another example of working towards integration comes from the work of adult psychoanalysts. The school of relational psychoanalysts in New York have been writing for some time about the importance of the relationship in psychoanalysis (Skolnick & Warshaw, 1992). Object relations theory is an important part of 'relational theory', but relational theorists have perhaps been rather more specific about the importance of external relationships. 'Relational theorists have in common an interest in the intrapsychic as well as the interpersonal, but the intrapsychic is seen as constituted largely by the internalisation of interpersonal experience mediated by the constraints imposed by biologically organized templates and delimiters' (Ghent, 1992, p. xviii). The school is looking to integrate different perspectives and was set up with that objective in mind. In the UK, a move to emphasise the relational in object relations theory can be seen in the work of Alvarez (1992), although she keeps the emphasis on internal object relations. Her work will be examined further in Chapter Two, because within her work on object relations theory (in which the concept of containment is embedded), she also uses the concept of reciprocity in her work with children with autism.

Dilys Daws was one of the pioneers of the Under 5's clinic at the Tavistock Clinic. The method underlying the work at this clinic can be seen in her book *Through the Night* (1993). Although this was written by a child psychotherapist working in a child psychotherapy clinic, the method described used containment, but also included a consideration of attunement. Daws did not use the concept of reciprocity as such, but she did use Stern's derived concept of attunement (Stern, 1985). Attunement was thought about in the later section of the book on the development of a sense of a separate self for the baby, rather than being posited as a core concept for the work, but Daws was very clear that the presence of the baby together with the parent/s is necessary for the work. She explained that this was required in order that she could observe the relationship between them, and it is difficult to imagine how this could not include a consideration of how 'in tune' the parents are with their baby and vice versa, even though this was not made explicit. My point is that the Under 5's clinic at the Tavistock was one of the first clinics to work with young children, and when the book was first published in 1989, it already showed that the methodology was becoming more integrative. For instance, Daws was looking at not only the baby and the relationship with the parents, but also the relationship between the parents and the relationship within the wider family, and this relates to the points made by Scavo, that the demands of work with infants and their parents require wider horizons from the therapists. Daws also included a behavioural analysis of the situation with her close questioning about the actual routines within the household. Behaviourism and psychotherapy are not usually natural bedfellows, but again the demands of the work may require that the therapist also integrates a practical behavioural approach within the psychotherapeutic context.

Balbernie (2003) has examined the research on a wide range of interventions with children under the age of five years. Although he concentrated on examining whether early, targeted interventions focused on the relationship can bring about long-term change, he also described a number of programmes where they have brought together different theoretical perspectives. It is interesting that he called them relationship-based services. In the UK, probably for various cultural reasons, interventions with young children have tended to be based on a behavioural model, apart from with some specialist professional groups, such as family therapists and child psychotherapists. However, programmes in other areas of the world have more clearly taken the relationship as the focus of their work. Watch, Wait and Wonder in Toronto (Cohen et al., 1999) uses a psychodynamic approach together with interactional guidance. These researchers compared 'traditional', non-directive parent–infant psychotherapy with Watch, Wait and Wonder, which uses a more directive technique, encouraging the parent to follow the play of the child and then exploring the feelings evoked in the session. The point I wish to make is not that one is better than the other. The results showed that the Watch, Wait and Wonder group achieved gains more quickly, but both achieved similar gains. Also, I think that 'traditional' parent–infant psychotherapy already uses a variety of interventions, based on different theories. However, these are not made explicit. My point is that interventions are emerging that *are* explicit in their use of different theoretical models all at once. Brazelton's Touchpoints programme in the USA (Brazelton, 2000) also uses a variety of approaches focused at 'touchpoints', those times of developmental progress where the child can become disorganised in a previously gained skill while trying to master a new one. In my view, this programme would gain both theoretically and practically if an understanding of containment were also included in it. Knowing about containment would have at least two applications. One is that if a baby had had experiences of trauma, the carer and practitioners would know that they had to be more active in containing the baby's anxiety. The other is that the practitioner would be aware of the need for containment of the mother. However, as discussed below, containment has tended to stay in the UK. McDonough's (2000) Interaction Guidance, an approach for difficult-to-engage families, integrates several theories, as does Marvin's attachment theory-based Circle of Security (Marvin et al., 2002). Both will be described later.

In their overview of interventions, Shonkoff and Phillips (2000) concluded: 'Programs that combine child-focussed educational activities with explicit attention to parent–child interaction patterns and relationship building appear to have the greatest impacts' (Shonkoff & Phillips, 2000, p. 379). They are therefore extending Balbernie's view, in that Balbernie was describing how programmes are developing that focus on relationships and integrating several theoretical models, but Shonkoff and Phillips conclude that programmes that focus on relationships are also the most effective.

This movement towards linking up concepts from different disciplines appears to be gathering pace, for instance, as described earlier by Shuttleworth (1999) on the eve of the third millennium.

However, there has been a long gestation over the past 30 or so years. There is already a close relationship between child psychotherapy and child development research. The child psychotherapy preclinical course includes child development research, such as research on the sentience of the foetus within the womb, the development of language in babies, and the reciprocity between the mother and baby. Later papers in the module bring together psychoanalytic theory and this research (e.g., Boston, 1991; Murray, 1991).

Some child development researchers have also been interested in bringing together their research with psychoanalytic theories. Daniel Stern, in his wide-ranging book (Stern, 1985), tried to integrate the two, pointing out that one of the psychoanalytic approaches, in his view, related well to the emerging data from child development research. 'The British object relations "school" and H. S. Sullivan, an American parallel, were unique among clinical theorists in believing that human social relatedness is present from birth, that it exists for its own sake, is of a definable nature and does not lean upon physiological need states' (Stern, 1985, p. 44). Other researchers also worked to bring the two bodies of knowledge together. The titles of two pieces of work illustrate this point: *Psychoanalysis and Infant Research*

(Lichtenberg, 1983) and '*New knowledge about the infant from current research: Implications for psychoanalysis*' (Brazelton, 1980).

I think it is no accident that these works were all written in the late 1970s and early 1980s by child development researchers. They were written following a rapid growth spurt in child development research. Clifton (2001), in her comprehensive review paper 'Lessons from infants: 1960–2000', pointed out that child development research on infants had seen an exponential growth between 1960 and 2000. Between 1960 and 1964, an average of 24 articles about infants were published per year. Between 1990 and 1995, an average of 1000 articles were published per year, so there has been more impetus to try to integrate these findings with previously established theories. This is because the escalation in the number of findings has increased the pressure to explain them. Psychoanalysts from the late nineteenth century onwards have had to speculate about the early life of the infant using their own observations, as other research data were not available. The fact that even by 1965 only 24 articles about infants were published per year attests to this. Now that more data are rapidly accruing, there is perhaps more of an opportunity to look at the relationship between these two bodies of knowledge.

However, bringing together two concepts from disparate areas has both negative and positive connotations. It is not easy to examine and link concepts from two fields in a way that is acceptable to both professional groups. Each concept is embedded within a rich literature of its own, known to the practitioners/researchers within that particular field. It can be difficult to explain the concept to another group not familiar with it and its context, and retain the complexity of it. Practitioners within that field may feel that 'their' concept has been 'watered down'. However, to refrain from attempting such an exercise would mean that whole groups of professionals would be unable to benefit from the potential of knowing about containment, while other groups would be unable to benefit from a knowledge of reciprocity. The irony is that each group is using the other's concept in practice, without naming it. For instance, as will be shown later, psychoanalytic psychotherapists are participating in reciprocal interactions within their practice. Ignoring this, when the concept is available, would make it more difficult to understand some clinical sessions and infant observations and would obviate the possibility of extending technique within sessions to include reciprocity as well as containment.

The examples quoted above relate to Hegel's idea about the thesis, antithesis and synthesis within the dialectic process, in that he stated that the development of ideas occurs within a historical time with its own particular pressures. Some of the pressures within our own time include, first, the creation of programmes to work with very young children, which, for the reasons outlined above by Scavo, are moving towards a more integrationist approach and, secondly, the growth of child development research on infants, which means that more knowledge is available about how and when infants relate to others. With all these related fields of research linked to containment and reciprocity, it is unlikely that the interrelationship between these two influential concepts can continue to be ignored. An examination of the concepts' relationship is likely to be useful to both practitioners and researchers, especially as each concept is influential within its own field.

Containment (Bion, 1959) is an extremely useful concept to inform work with infants and young children, and it is at the heart of publications arising out of the Tavistock Under 5's model of working (e.g., Daws, 1993). It is also a core concept for psychoanalysis. In Hinshelwood's words, it is 'a decisive concept for most British forms of analytic psychotherapy' (Hinshelwood, 1991, p. 246). Reciprocity (Brazelton et al., 1974) is an influential concept and has a central place in the field of child development research. However, because these two concepts have grown up in separate disciplines with different research traditions, it is not clear whether or how they relate to each other, even though each is very important within its own discipline.

I think, however, that containment and reciprocity refer to phenomena that do have a relationship to each other and that both co-exist within the psychoanalytic work in the therapy room, as I hope to demonstrate in the following pages. Both concepts highlight fundamental processes that enable us to relate to each other. I also think that these two phenomena are the fundamental building blocks underpinning the quality of an attachment and, therefore, that it may be possible to change both relationships and the quality of an attachment through interventions using them.

Psychoanalytic and child development concepts, together with concepts in many other domains, are formulated, subsequently applied in practice, and then described in the literature. They are continually shaped and extended in the interplay between practice and theoretical examination. For instance, it has been through the work of clinicians in the clinical room that the concept of containment has been described and developed since Bion first described it in 1959. Bion originally used the example of a mother–infant interaction to formulate his concept of containment (Bion, 1959), but his subsequent writing concentrated on containment as applied to a theory of thinking, to the learning process, to containment of oneself, and to adult–adult interaction. Although he first used his imagined interaction of the mother and infant, he was an analyst of adults and did not study or work with children. However, his initial description of containment resonated with child analysts and child psychotherapists, and they began to incorporate his idea when describing their interactions in the clinical room. Thus, the concept was mainly shaped through clinical papers, in the interplay between formulation and application.

Similarly, reciprocity was postulated by Brazelton in 1974, and, even though reciprocity was described more comprehensively in his original paper than when Bion originally described containment, the concept of reciprocity has been developed through further research and observations reported in the literature. In order to study the concepts, therefore, it has been necessary to study the literature. I will present and examine vignettes from child development literature to show that the phenomena of containment can be seen to occur within the descriptions of the interaction between an adult and infant, even though the explanatory concept is not used and may not even be known about by the observer/writer. Likewise, I will also present descriptions of clinical sessions by child psychotherapists to show that the phenomena of reciprocity can be seen to be occurring. Analysing the vignettes also begins to elucidate the relationship between the two concepts: the concepts are different but there is a relationship, and it is quite surprising how closely linked they are.

In order to generate a definition of the two concepts, the original papers related to each of the two concepts were examined to identify the presence or absence of a definition, Brazelton et al. (1974) for the concept of reciprocity and Bion (1959) for the concept of containment. As Bion did not define containment, describing it in a diffuse way, dictionaries of psychoanalysis were consulted for a definition of containment. None included a definition, so a detailed examination of a contemporary series of books published by a leading psychoanalytic psychotherapeutic organisation, the Tavistock Clinic, was carried out in order to find descriptions of the concept of containment in contemporary use. Publications by the Tavistock Clinic were chosen because they are widely representative of a cross-section of people who use the concept of containment, that is, child psychoanalysts and child psychotherapists and clinicians who work in both the public and private sectors. A definition was then forged from the elements within the publications.

Brazelton did not define reciprocity, but he had written extensively about it within his paper, providing sufficient detail to generate a definition. Reciprocity has been a very fruitful concept. Other researchers have developed ideas arising from it, Colwyn Trevarthen on intersubjectivity (Trevarthen, 1980), Edward Tronick on mutual affect regulation (Tronick et al., 1986), and Daniel Stern on attunement (Stern, 1985). Trevarthen, who developed the idea of intersubjectivity, worked with Brazelton while Brazelton carried out and analysed his research. Brazelton concentrated on the interaction within the mother–infant dyads, while Trevarthen analysed the interaction between the infant and inanimate objects. I have the impression that both Tronick and Stern knew Brazelton personally at that time as well as being aware of his work. Each child development researcher can be seen as developing particular aspects of reciprocity, according to their interests, as each researcher has a different emphasis. I will try to clarify some of the differences between attunement, mutual affect regulation and intersubjectivity. I will also use some of the ideas to show how it is possible to envisage a continuum of reciprocity and how this continuum relates to containment.

I will also cite research which indicates that reciprocity and containment are the mechanisms involved in creating the quality of an attachment. The implication of this, is that in interventions it should be possible to change the quality of an attachment by using both reciprocity and containment, and I will show that some current interventions that are explicitly based on attachment theory explicitly or implicitly use reciprocity and implicitly use containment.

2 Has anyone else looked at integrating these two concepts?

I have outlined some evidence in the previous chapter to show that there is a movement to integrate different theories when working with infants and their families. However, there is a dearth of work in both the psychodynamic and the child development literature examining specific links between containment and reciprocity. This chapter will outline the attempts to bring together different theoretical strands and research from different areas where there are links to containment/reciprocity, but it is a short chapter because there is a lack of directly relevant work!

The main writer who has already pointed out the need for reciprocity to be linked to psychoanalytic thinking is Anne Alvarez. I am developing this idea by showing in detail that there is a relationship between reciprocity and the most influential psychoanalytic concept, containment, and that the two can be used together to illuminate any relationship. In her influential book (Alvarez, 1992), she quotes widely from Brazelton's paper (Brazelton et al., 1974). Although Alvarez is using autism as the lens through which she examines Bion's concepts, she reaches the conclusion that a particular element within reciprocity needs to be added to object relations theory.

> It is in the particular area of the alerting and amplifying activities which Brazelton describes that I feel our psychoanalytic theories may need enlarging if they are to be relevant to the treatment of the illest of psychotic children.
>
> (Alvarez, 1992, p. 68)

She points out that a mother is more than just a container and a baby is more than a seeker after the satisfaction of bodily needs. She uses the work of Wolff (1965) to show that the baby seeks new experiences.

Wolff used physiological measures of alert inactivity, characterised by a 'bright shiny look in the eye', to show that these periods of alert watchfulness occurred when the baby was physically comfortable after a feed or after defecation. Thus, the baby is born with a readiness to learn that is not dependent on the satisfaction of other drives. Alvarez linked this piece of child development research with the psychoanalytic concept developed by Bion, that of K (Bion, 1962a).

Bion attempted to develop a theory of thinking. He postulated that there are different kinds of thoughts and precursors to thoughts. He defined K as an activity, 'in the K activity on which I am engaged, namely in knowing' (Bion, 1962a, p. 50), the type of thinking that is curious and wants to know more. He distinguished between knowing something and knowing about something. 'Knowing something consists in "having" some "piece of" knowledge and not in what I have called K . . . "knowing" in the sense of getting to know something' (Bion, 1962a, p. 65). He also used this in the context of the relationship between the mother and baby, in that the mother could have loving or hating thoughts about her baby, but she could also have 'K' thoughts, wanting to know about the state of mind of her baby. He thought that 'the earliest and most primitive manifestation of K occurs in the relationship between mother and infant' (Bion, 1962a, p. 90) and that both the mother and the baby achieved 'mental growth' through this activity.

Alvarez used Wolff's research and Klein's (Klein, 1930) and Bion's theoretical development to postulate that babies show a need to get to know the world, the epistemological instinct, from birth. She builds on Bion's idea of an innate preconception of a psychological object, meeting together with a realisation to create a conception of something; that is, that we have innate pre-programmed ideas (preconception) that we are not aware of, that turn into a known idea (conception) when we see/meet the idea in reality (realisation). Alvarez further integrated the work of Wolff, Bion and others to propose that babies are 'innately *prepared for*, and innately *requiring*, a relationship with an intelligent being, and able to respond *when this being creates the right preconditions*' (Alvarez, 1992, p. 199). This view is supported by both earlier and current child development research, which will be discussed in more detail later.

I think that Bion's idea would benefit from a fourth stage, moving through a preconception to a realisation to a concept to a fourth stage of 'naming', in that it may be that we have a preconception of containment and reciprocity, which we see all the time in the interactions of people together (realisations), and it may be that they become concepts, something we know about within ourselves. But in order to have the concept available to conscious thought and therefore be able to notice, identify and use it in our work, I think it requires another stage of 'naming'. This arises from my experience of teaching experienced health visitors how to use containment and reciprocity in their work. Most have never heard of either concept, even though it would capture processes which occur frequently in their work. However, many are able to grasp the rudiments of the concepts after a brief explanation and are then able to recognise them both in their past and present work. The point about naming is that it allows for generalisation to new situations. Without this naming, however, the concepts are not available to conscious thought (cf. Wittgenstein, 1921) and their use in practice may be minimised. This fourth stage has also been alluded to by Williams (1998), where she describes the functions of the containing object; it 'receives the projections and attempts . . . to give them a name, modify them and make them thinkable' (Williams, 1998, p. 95). This is also the point of this book, in that naming both containment and reciprocity for different scientific communities allows both concepts to be used and the phenomena to be recognised across situations.

Urban (1999) did not use the concept of reciprocity, but she did try to bring together child development research with psychoanalytic theory. She proposed that identificatory processes precede projective identification. She quoted Fordham, who, late in his work, concluded: 'At first an infant has not enough structure for projective identification to occur without an earlier period in which identity between subject and object predominates' (Astor, 1995, p. 61). She used the concept of transmodal perception, where sensations are amodal, that is, do not belong to only one sense, but translate across senses (Meltzoff & Borton, 1979). Emotion is transmodal and transpersonal.

> An infant directly perceives, say, the mother's feeling of goodness when she talks to him, and apprehends the perceived goodness in her voice to be the same as his own experience of goodness. What is relevant to the infant is the categorical affect of 'goodness' and its contour and intensity. It is irrelevant to him that two people are experiencing it
>
> (Urban, 1999, p. 2)

The change from amodal to featural perception seems to occur at around five months of age (Bower, 1982). Urban referred to another piece of child development research, that of Meltzoff and Moore

(1989), who showed that an infant, as well as being able to imitate another's expression, can carry on the imitation after the other's face has disappeared, implying that short-term memory is active and that the perception has moved into being a representation. Gergely (1991) suggested that emotions link similar experiences together, which then form into a representation. These representations could be the beginnings of good and bad objects, the creations of internal objects. Urban has attempted to discover whether something precedes projective identification, and her integration of child development research with object relations theory to propose a mechanism for the creation of internal objects is interesting.

Other child psychotherapists have included an appreciation of reciprocity or the related theories of attunement, intersubjectivity and mutual affect regulation in their work – Besnard et al. (1998) and Reid (1997), whose work will be discussed in more detail later. Likierman (2003) applied the thinking from parent–infant psychotherapy to depressed women, taking an integrative approach using 'findings from psychoanalytic theory, infancy research, evolutionary biology and anthropology' (Likierman, 2003, p. 301). Within this, she specifically mentions the work of Brazelton and Tronick on reciprocal relationships. However, these child psychotherapists remain in the minority at present. Those who are integrating this aspect of child development research into their practice tend to be those who work with children under five years old or those who are involved with infant observation. Infant observation describes the situation where a person observes an infant for up to an hour. The process has been described by Miller et al. (1989). The infant can be alone or with his/her family. This observation is then written up in great detail and is often discussed within a small group of other observers. It allows an appreciation of the capacities of infants, their relationships and their emotional development. As has been discussed previously, it can be no accident that it is those working with very young children who are integrating these concepts.

Within the child psychotherapeutic community in the UK, Alvarez (1992), Likierman (2003), Daws (1993), Besnard (1998) and Reid (1997) have included reciprocity-related theories in their work. However, even though others may well have mentioned reciprocity or reciprocity-related theories, they are in a minority and the literature is minimal. To date, no writers have specifically considered how the two concepts of containment and reciprocity relate to each other, even though these concepts are hugely influential within their field.

Most of the literature that is working towards a broad integration of approaches or theories comes from the USA, perhaps because practitioners and researchers there have been working and publishing in the field of infant mental health longer and more prolifically than in any other country, and, as has been pointed out before, working with infants and their families seems to push the need for integration (Scavo, 2000). Music (2004) in his review of Altman's work on relational child psychotherapy in the USA (Altman et al., 2002) points out how the relational perspective in the USA has been influenced by child development research and various psychoanalytic perspectives. However, this type of literature tends to integrate broad approaches. Beebe (2003) pointed out that there are two main categories of intervention in parent–infant work: psychodynamic and interactional/ behavioural, with the behavioural concentrating on the interaction between the mother and infant. Her work integrates both approaches, and she cites others who are also working towards integrating different approaches. This includes Stern (1995), Seligman (1994), Lieberman et al. (2000), Greenspan (1981), Bakermans-Kranenburg et al. (1998) Hofacker and Papousek (1998) and Cramer (1998). The work of Alicia Lieberman and her colleagues will be used to illustrate this type of integration.

Lieberman and her colleagues considered the core concepts and current approaches within infant–parent psychotherapy. They used the term 'multimodal' therapy to describe parent–infant psychotherapy, pointing out that it uses both interpretive and supportive techniques. Interpretation is the classical ingredient of psychoanalytic psychotherapy, while supportive techniques are used by many other therapies. Psychoanalytic psychotherapies are supposed not to use these supportive techniques, although Wallerstein's psychotherapy research project in 1986 found that psychoanalytic therapy in the USA did include more supportive elements than their practitioners realised. Lieberman outlined the influences on parent–infant psychotherapy as 'relational theories, such as attachment theory, American intersubjective theory, British object relations theory, self psychology and current trends in Freudian theory' (Lieberman et al., 2000, p. 475). It is interesting that they characterise object relations theory as British and intersubjective theories as American; that is, containment from object relations theory is a British concept and reciprocity as an intersubjective theory is American. This is a slight oversimplification, as one of the main intersubjective theorists is Colwyn Trevarthen, who is British and whose concept is, aptly, called intersubjectivity (Trevarthen, 1980). However, the other main theorists are American – Brazelton et al. (1974) for reciprocity, Tronick et al. (1986) for mutual affect regulation, and Stern (1985) for attunement – and their concepts will be considered in more detail later. Lieberman concluded that the 'therapeutic relationship is a basic catalyst for change, and it becomes the vehicle for utilizing a combination of intervention modalities that include insight-oriented psychotherapy, unstructured developmental guidance, emotional support, and concrete assistance as well as crisis intervention when needed' (Lieberman et al., 2000, p. 483).

Lombardi and Lapidos (1990) attempted to integrate infant research with clinical practice, but their paper is mentioned as another example of this endeavour rather than as a successful example. The authors seem unaware of the British literature on psychoanalytic work with children, as they state that 'the use of countertransference in work with children has a somewhat different cast, and literature on the subject is particularly sparse' (Lombardi & Lapidos, 1990, p. 90). However, the British object relations school has a rich literature on the use of counter-transference in the publications from over 40 years of the *Journal of Child Psychotherapy* and the *International Journal of Infant Observation*.

Alvarez (1992) thought that aspects of object relations theory were being included by child development researchers. She suggested that 'a modified object-relations theory with an understanding of primitive or minimal objects, or pre-objects, and with distinctions between preconceptions and concepts is . . . already in existence in the work of Klein, Bion and infant development researchers' (Alvarez, 1992, p. 199). This is interesting because, as pointed out earlier, she wants reciprocity, a child development concept, linked to psychoanalytic thinking, and in this quotation she is suggesting that the reverse is already happening, that some elements of object relations theory are already being included within child development research.

Murray (1991) brought together object relations theory and inter-subjectivity, the concept related to reciprocity, to explain some of the disruption she found in the relationship of women with post-natal depression and their infants. She compared the interaction of depressed women and their infants with a control group. A series of questionnaires was administered, and a subsample of mothers with their infants were filmed interacting for five minutes, from the age of two months old up to 18 months old. The mothers were asked to play with their babies without using toys for five minutes. Murray found that depressed mothers were more preoccupied with their own experience than with their infants' experience, and this meant that the mothers did not engage in the to and fro of a reciprocal interaction with their babies. They 'expressed more hostility towards their infants and were less likely to acknowledge the infant as an active subject or agent' (Murray, 1991, p. 228). These infants then performed less well on a number of measures at the age of 18 months than the control group. An adverse outcome was not related to the duration of the depression or its severity. An adverse outcome was related to 'where the mother's speech had shown a preoccupation with her own experience rather than with the infant's . . . it was this feature of the mother's interaction with the infant that accounted for the poor performance of infants of depressed women' (Murray, 1991, p. 228).

Murray used both object relations theory and intersubjectivity to emphasise 'the importance of the quality of maternal engagement for infant mental health development' (Murray, 1991, p. 229). Murray's paper utilised several concepts within object relations theory, although containment was only briefly considered. Reciprocity and intersubjectivity were considered within the paper, but only with regard to how they illuminate the mother–infant relationship. The relationship between containment and reciprocity was not examined.

One heroic attempt to try to integrate current different theoretical strands is that by Schore (e.g., Schore, 2003), who has integrated an enormous amount of research from neuroscience with child development research, attachment theory and projective identification. His work will be discussed later. The huge increase in research on infancy and on neuroscience must have the corollary that it is now difficult for even an expert in the field to keep up to date with all the findings.

Lieberman et al. (2000) pointed out that there was a paradigm shift in the 1970s, from a 'unidirectional examination of the parent's influence on the child to a bi-directional model of reciprocal influences' (p. 476). Trevarthen, commenting on Brazelton's research, put it another way. He 'had not realised, at least as a scientist, how expressive and how sensitive a baby could be' (Trevarthen, 1980, p. 317); that is, that the baby is as active as the parent. The fulcrum for the paradigm shift, in my view, was Brazelton's work, published in 1974, which showed that *both* the parent and the baby were active in relating to each other.

These writers all represent a move away from the old 'either/or' argument and a move towards a 'both/and' approach, integrating varying concepts in practice. They also represent Hegel's philosophy in action, moving through a dialectical process of contrasting different approaches, the thesis and the antithesis, to integrating them, the synthesis. There is a growing number of researchers and clinicians who are synthesising different methods, as required by the demands of the work. However, there are very few examples of the conscious combined use of containment and reciprocity, and there is almost nothing written about how these two concepts relate to each other.

3 What is containment?

The origin of the concept

'The more successfully the word and its use can be "established" the more its precision becomes an obstructive rigidity; the more imprecise it is, the more it is a stumbling-block to comprehension' (Bion, 1970, p. 80). It is fitting to begin with Bion's words, as this section will define Bion's concept of containment, something which he seems to have avoided doing, perhaps purposefully in the light of the above quotation.

Bion began working at the Tavistock Clinic in 1932 as a psychiatrist, and then started his training in London as an adult psychoanalyst in 1945, with Melanie Klein as his analyst. He moved to Los Angeles in 1968. He was a very creative man, who was able to work with an adult, but extrapolate his thoughts back in time to imagine the situation for that person as an infant.

Bion developed the concept of containment, but did not define it. Perhaps his way of walking a tightrope between being too precise and too imprecise enabled the psychoanalytical community to use and develop his idea so fruitfully.

Although it is an influential concept, Bion alludes to it almost in passing, rather than concentrating or elaborating on it. All of his writings on containment cover only a few pages. He developed the concept in a diffuse manner, over time and in several different places within his work. However, even though containment has never been elaborated upon at a theoretical level, it has been accessible to practitioners to the extent of the concept's becoming an extremely influential one.

Words and their meaning evolve and change over time, as people use them, and it will be interesting to examine whether the concept of containment has developed over time as I examine Bion's original writings and then a range of more contemporary practitioners.

Even though Bion did not define containment, it would have been helpful to begin this section with a generally accepted definition of it. However, finding such a definition has not been possible. *A Dictionary of Kleinian Thought* (Hinshelwood, 1991) describes some of Bion's thinking about it, without defining it, and *The Language of Psychoanalysis* considers projective identification without mentioning containment (Laplanche & Pontalis, 1988). *The Dictionary of the Work of W. R. Bion* (Lopez-Corvo, 2003) has surprisingly little on containment, just two and a half pages on container–contained, with no definition of containment. Considering that this is Bion's most influential concept, it is surprising that so little space is devoted to it. The same amount of space is given to Bion's view of 'common sense', which has had little general impact on the thinking of psychotherapists, unlike containment.

As it has not been possible to find a generally available definition of containment, a definition will be provided after considering Bion's writing and others' work in this field.

The genesis of containment lies in projection, a concept which was developed by Freud. 'It expels whatever within itself becomes a source of unpleasure . . . the mechanism of projection' (Freud, 1915/1991, p. 133). Projection means that a person externalises his own emotion in someone else as a way of not accepting it in himself. For instance, someone might feel angry but not want to admit it to himself, so he might then externalise his anger in others, seeing them as angry. 'He takes such pains to transpose outwards what becomes troublesome to him from within – that is to *project* it' (Freud, 1917/1991, p. 241).

In turn, Klein (1946) elaborated on projection and generated the concept of projective identification.

> Much of the hatred against parts of the self is now directed towards the mother. This leads to a particular form of identification which establishes the prototype of an aggressive object-relation. I suggest for these processes the term 'projective identification'. When projection is mainly derived from the infant's impulse to harm or control the mother, he feels her to be a persecutor. In psychotic disorders this identification of an object with the hated parts of the self contributes to the intensity of the hatred directed against other people.
>
> (Klein, 1946/1988, p. 8)

In other words, projective identification means that a person projects an aspect of himself into someone else, an action that Klein and other analysts at that time thought of as a mechanism to rid the self of that aspect. Bion later described and emphasised the role of projective identification as a way of trying to communicate particularly painful or difficult feelings. The 'identification' section of projective identification means that the person identifies with the feeling in the other person.

> Klein's new idea that these internal contents are projected 'into' an object implied in turn that the object is gradually felt to contain the infant's internal contents or parts. The infant necessarily begins to equate the object with disowned aspects of himself, and so direct all his self-hatred on to the misrecognised object.
>
> (Likierman, 2001, p. 156)

For example, a mother may project her own feeling of being unlovable into her baby and then identify with her baby as unloved and unlovable. Bion explains projective identification as follows:

> The nature of the functions which excite the patient's curiosity he explores by projective identification. His own feelings, too powerful to be contained within his personality, are among these functions. Projective identification makes it possible for him to investigate his own feelings in a personality powerful enough to contain them.
>
> (Bion, 1959/1993, p. 106)

In this passage, Bion is linking projective identification to containment. He developed the idea that projective identification is not just utilised in the service of destructiveness, but is also a communication (Bion, 1962a).

Bion developed this idea to create the concept of containment, the container/contained. The first appearance of this idea was in 1959. Substantial quotations have been included from this first material, because of the dearth of material on containment from his original writings, and so that the source can be examined. He started with a description of projective identification:

> When the patient strove to rid himself of fears of death which were felt to be too powerful for his personality to contain he split off his fears and put them into me, the idea apparently being that

if they were allowed to repose there long enough they would undergo modification by my psyche and could then be safely reintrojected.

(Bion, 1959/1993, p. 103)

Here Bion begins to approach the 'how' of containment, the mechanism of it. Introjection is the opposite of projection, in that instead of projecting something out, something is taken into the psyche. He uses the word 'contain', although here the context is the patient who cannot contain. However, in the use of the negative, he moves to a consideration of the positive, in that if there is one who cannot contain, that implies the existence of one who can contain. The segment 'repose there long enough they would undergo modification' already suggests the idea of containment.

He develops the idea of lack of containment later in the paragraph, where he considers the mother–infant relationship.

The analytic situation built up in my mind a sense of witnessing an extremely early scene. I felt that the patient had witnessed in infancy a mother who had dutifully responded to the infant's emotional displays. The dutiful response had in it an element of impatient 'I don't know what's the matter with the child'. My deduction was that in order to understand what the child wanted the mother should have treated the infant's cry as more than a demand for her presence. From the infant's point of view she should have taken into her, and thus experienced, the fear that the child was dying. It was this fear that the child could not contain. He strove to split it off together with the part of the personality in which it lay and project it into the mother. An understanding mother is able to experience the feeling of dread that this baby was striving to deal with by projective identification, and yet retain a balanced outlook. This patient had had to deal with a mother who could not tolerate experiencing such feelings and reacted either by denying them ingress, or alternatively by becoming a prey to the anxiety which resulted from introjection of the baby's bad feelings.

(Bion, 1959/1993, p. 104)

Here he writes about the baby trying to project emotion as well as part of the personality into the mother. His assumption is that perhaps the baby is unable to distinguish between itself and its emotions so tries to get rid of both. However, he does not write that the mother actually introjects part of the baby's personality. When he writes on behalf of the mother, he refers only to feelings. Earlier, when referring to his patient, he stated that the patient projected his fears, not part of his personality. I am emphasising this point, as it will become relevant later when considering whether or when containment refers to emotions or parts of the personality.

He then moves on to comment on the importance of the mother's being able to have a sense of the baby's feeling without being overwhelmed by the emotion. In this example, he does not specifically develop the next stage of the baby's reintrojecting an emotion made tolerable, but he does make it explicit in his example of the patient. However, it is interesting how he writes about the next stage, because he does not say that his (Bion's) psyche modifies the emotions and then these modified emotions can be reintrojected. He says that this is the patient's idea. However, he does imply it when describing the mother–baby interaction, in that the mother needs to experience the intensity of the emotion but modify *her* experience of it so that she is able to 'retain a balanced outlook'. I am pointing out these distinctions because, theoretically, they are interesting. There are two distinctions to be considered. The first distinction is whether theorists are postulating that it is emotions that are projected out or whether it is part of the personality. The second distinction is whether it is 'as if' emotions (or the part of the personality) are projected out, rather than that they are actually put in the other person. This will be considered as we look at the way the concept is currently used.

Contemporary use of containment

An examination of Bion's writings has given a glimpse of containment from his point of view. Unfortunately, as has been pointed out, dictionaries of psychotherapeutic terms do not include a definition of containment at present. It may be interesting to examine more modern usage of the concept to see whether a current meaning emerges. I have chosen a series of writings, published as a series in 1997 and 1998, and all published from the Tavistock Clinic, in order to take a snapshot at a particular time and with the stamp of a leading institution. The Tavistock Clinic represents a cross-section of child psychotherapists and analysts working in both the public and private sectors.

Garland (1998) translated Bion as follows:

> He linked what the mother can do for the baby with what the therapist can do for the patient: help transform the unbearable

into something that can eventually be thought about . . . rather than responded to as an overwhelming experience that causes a further breakdown of the ability to think.

(Garland, 1998, p. 110)

Although Garland is writing about adult trauma, specifically rape, it is interesting that she begins a description of containment by referring to the mother–baby relationship:

> Containment is a fundamental of what goes on between a mother and baby. It means that the mother can grasp the importance of, and take into herself, some of the baby's earliest and most primitive anxieties. . . . She can think about such things in her own way without being caught up in them, overwhelmed by them herself. Babies with mothers who can take the panic out of their anxieties, eventually take into themselves some version of a mother who can manage – who can get hold of something important emotionally without being knocked off balance by it. Eventually the baby takes into itself . . . the mother's capacity to tolerate and manage anxiety.
>
> (Garland, 1998, p. 109)

Anderson (1998) explained containment in the following way:

> In early life, the baby achieves a sense of psychological holding and safety by having a mother who can be in a state of openness to the baby's state of mind called reverie. The baby can . . . communicate primitive anxiety to the mother who, in a quite intuitive way, drawing on her own inner resources including her past experience of maternal care, receives these feelings. She copes with them, is open to them, is affected by them, but is not overwhelmed by them. . . . If the mother can manage such fears, then she communicates this back to the baby in her own language – the tone of her voice, the manner of holding, a look in the eyes, and the baby then has an experience of relief, of someone who could manage something that he cannot. Gradually, after many experiences like this, the baby can learn to tolerate primitive states of mind. Thus containment functions as a way of detoxifying the baby's primitive experiences.
>
> (Anderson, 1998, p. 73)

Anderson then talks about how a failure of containment can lead to other ways of trying to deal with anxiety, including projective identification 'ridding the self of a dangerous world' (Anderson, 1998, p. 74).

Waddell (1998) described Bion's thoughts as follows:

> The mother becomes the 'container' and the baby's fragmentary impulses and emotions, the 'contained'. The container/contained relationship constitutes Bion's model for the thinking of thoughts, a model for processing emotional experience which . . . makes a fundamental contribution to the structuring of the personality.
>
> (Waddell, 1998, p. 32)

Williams (1997) defined a container as a 'person able to receive into herself . . . a chaotic input of feelings and sensations, mainly painful ones' (p. 26). This quotation emphasises an aspect of the concept of containment that differs from reciprocity. Containment tends to emphasise 'negative', distressing emotions.

Dubinsky (1997) wrote that

> The name of containment is usually given to the relationship described by Bion as that between 'container' and 'contained'. This concept is an abstraction based on the model of a mother (the container) who, through her comprehension, transforms the painful projections (the contained) from her baby in such a way that the baby can then introject them back into a tolerable form.
>
> (Dubinsky, 1997, p. 7)

Before examining these quotations, I am going to conclude with an earlier quotation from Daws (1991). I am concluding with her work because she takes the definitions a step further in that, as well as considering the mother and baby, she also succinctly links the work between mother and baby together with the practitioner. Bion transposed in time the work, likening the containment between mother and baby to that between analyst and analysand, but Daws, in her work with infants, brings the whole process together as she works with the two generations at once.

> Containing a baby's anxiety is difficult just because it so easily connects with parents' own anxieties. . . . Talking through these fears and experiences makes them more manageable. When the mother meets the baby's anxiety in the night it no longer connects

with her own infinite dread and she can respond to it appropriately. It seems as though my work involves directly containing the mother's anxiety so that she can go back to the baby and contain it for the baby.

(Daws, 1991, p. 116)

In her description, Garland includes the next stage of containment, where the baby, from his experience, is able to internalise the experience of being contained and develops his own ability or 'internal container' to contain or process his emotions. 'Eventually the baby takes into itself . . . the mother's capacity to tolerate and manage anxiety' (Garland, 1998, p. 109).

I would like to make two points, which sound somewhat esoteric but may be of interest to those concerned with the finer points of psychoanalytic theory! The first is about what is projected and the second is about the nature of projection. Firstly, the striking feature of all these contemporary explanations of containment is that none of them refer to parts of the self or parts of the personality, but most of them refer to anxiety or emotion, apart from Dubinsky, who refers to 'painful projections' and is writing about psychosis. I think that because Bion's idea of containment is very close to Klein's theory of projective identification, the idea of projecting out part of the personality or self is woven through his piece of material. However, it is also striking that Bion emphasises fear and anxiety, and at the end of the quotation from Bion (1959), the author uses 'feelings' as a description of what is projected. The current use of projection for those working with children therefore appears to be largely with regard to emotions rather than to parts of the self or personality. However, there may be a difference of emphasis between adult analysts and those working with children. Adult analysts may refer more to parts of the self, perhaps because adult analysis emphasises a consideration of the personality. Perhaps in adults the personality is more formed, and adults would like to rid themselves of part of the self, whereas the personality is more fluid in young children and children attempt to dismiss feelings rather than parts of the self. Thus, child psychotherapists may find themselves working more with emotions.

Secondly, with regard to whether the emotion/self is actually projected into someone else or whether it is as if it is projected, I think that for both parts of the self and emotions it is 'as if' they are projected outwards. Recent research on mirror neurons (Keysers et al., 2003) demonstrated that physical activity in one primate when perceived by an observing primate caused the same electrical activity in the brain of the observer as in the actor. Although the emotions are not literally flung out by one person to be gathered up by another, there are many mechanisms through which we get a sense of what another is feeling. As well as observation of the many non-verbal phenomena through which we sense what another feels – such as facial expression, tone of voice, eye contact, body posture, etc. (Ekman, 1983; Zajonc, 1985) – it may be that the perception of emotion in the actor also leads to similar brain activity in the observer, contributing to the experience of a shared emotion. Therefore, I think that for both self and emotions it is 'as if' they are projected outward, but that the observer can have an experience of the other's emotion through these mechanisms.

Moreover, the idea of these 'as if' situations is supported by Bion's later writings. The idea behind projection is that it is as if an emotion is removed by projecting it outward. In his lectures in São Paulo (Bion, 1990), Bion seems very clear that it is not that an emotion is concretely put into someone else; it is more of an 'as if' situation. I have emphasised six words in the following passage to show that here Bion is writing about an 'as if' situation:

> Suppose the mother picks up the baby and comforts it, is not at all disorganised or distressed, but makes some soothing response. The distressed infant *can feel that*, by its screams or yells, it has expelled those feelings of impending disaster into the mother. The mother's response *can be felt* to detoxicate the evacuation of the infant; the sense of impending disaster is modified by the mother's reaction and can then be taken back into itself by the baby.
>
> (Bion, 1990, p. 43)

Perhaps this is a movement from early Bion to late Bion, in that earlier, in 1959, he talked about his patient taking his fear and 'the part of the personality in which it lay' and 'project[ing] it into the mother', but later, in 1990, he refers only to emotions and that it is 'as if' these are actually projected out into another person. This movement was a historical development over time.

The definition of containment

I am therefore going to take the definition of containment from the middle part of the spectrum, because most contemporary writers refer to emotions, rather than parts of the self. The emotions of anxiety, fear and terror are included within the spectrum of emotional communications. These are the emotions often worked with by therapists. The definition is as follows:

> Containment is thought to occur when one person receives and understands the emotional communication of another without being overwhelmed by it, processes it and then communicates understanding and recognition back to the other person. This process can restore the capacity to think in the other person.

A note on previous views of containment

This definition of containment has been generated through a consideration of contemporary writers' views. However, it is also worth bearing in mind that there have been other emphases made on the concept of containment in the past in other publications from the Tavistock Clinic. For example, Esther Bick, who instituted the observation of infants at the Tavistock Clinic in 1948, emphasised the soothing or calming aspect of containment:

> The need for a containing object would seem, in the infantile unintegrated state, to produce a frantic search for an object – a light, a voice, a smell, or other sensual object – which can hold the attention and thereby be experienced, momentarily at least, as holding the parts of the personality together.
>
> (Bick, 1968, p. 188)

In a way, she alludes to a pre-projection phase, where the baby feels as though he is falling apart, but is unable to project. This phase also precedes the ability to split or to use paranoid-schizoid functioning: 'The stage of primal splitting and idealization of self and object can now be seen to rest on this earlier process of containment of self and object by their respective "skins"' (Bick, 1968, p. 187).

The containment continuum

However, to return to current thinking and in order to integrate part of Bion's original idea while also moving towards a post-Bion development, it may be helpful to propose a containment continuum. This will also be discussed in more detail later. At one end, with projective identification in full flow, is containment with the idea of containing parts of the self or personality, albeit as an 'as if' situation. This could be called 'macro-containment'. The projection of parts of the self may occur more in psychotic functioning, or where there are greater disturbances in mental health and personality development. Then, in the middle, is the idea of containing fears, anxieties and emotions with high affect and then to 'micro-containment' at the other end of the spectrum (this is linked to mutual affect regulation, which will be explained later as one element in the process of reciprocity).

Restoring the capacity to think

The final section of the definition alludes to the restoration of the capacity to think, an extremely important outcome of the successful process of containment. The examples quoted from Waddell (1998) and Garland (1998) show that, although one aspect of containment is to be able to process emotion, both Waddell and Garland highlight another aspect: that is, that containment restores the ability to think. The research explaining the organic foundation for this may already exist and will be considered later. One idea about thinking and containment is reflected in the work of Britton (1989); that is, that thinking requires a space in which thoughts can be thought about. Bion thought that the idea of the container–contained implied the creation of a space for thought, and Britton described another space as being created by the Oedipal triangle. Both these accounts can sound rather concrete, implying an actual space within a container. However, to some degree, this is probably the case if the brain is seen as the container, in that when the brain is bathed in too high a level of stress hormones, such as cortisol and adrenalin and the more primitive levels of the brain are rampant, the ability to think within the 'higher functioning' cortex becomes impaired (e.g., Schore, 1994), and there is literally no space to think. This will be considered in more detail later. At a more symbolic level, when one's mind is taken up with strong feelings, there is not much room left for rational thought. Therefore, although the process of containment is important for the quality of life, implying a relationship between two people and providing the wherewithal to process and integrate emotional experience, the result of containment occurring is also important, in that the ability to think, solve problems and create is also integral to the development of quality in our lives and is the cornerstone of mental health.

The limits of influence of the concept of containment

So, having generated a definition, we can move on to consider what impact the concept of containment has had, before examining in more detail the link to the ability to think and describing some possible organic bases for containment. Writers on the history of science have sometimes looked at how a particular theory or scientific finding has become known by others. For example, Latour (1983) examined the particular forces at work that helped promulgate Pasteur's work on vaccination. These included an anthrax outbreak, Pasteur's ability to liaise with different sections of society in order to promote his ideas, and his ability to showcase his work and disseminate the results. He staged a public demonstration of the strength of his vaccine at Pouilly-le-Fort farm, assembling the press on three occasions to observe the results of vaccinating or not vaccinating. Different forces are always at work, so that some theories are better known than others. Various forces are also affecting the use of the concept of containment.

Containment is 'a decisive concept for most British forms of analytical psychotherapy' (Hinshelwood, 1991, p. 246). However, the telling word here is 'British'. Laplanche and Pontalis (1988), in their French dictionary of psychoanalysis, do not refer to containment. Other English-language nations, such as the USA, hardly refer to containment. Within the UK, other professional groups who work with children and their families, within the health service, education and social services, have never heard of 'containment'. Yet it is an illuminating and very useful concept in that it can explain and direct part of the therapeutic interaction within a session or part of an interaction between parent and infant, as well as informing the training of therapists. There are probably many reasons why this state of affairs exists, but perhaps one is the lack of writing concentrating on containment itself. Mostly, it is woven through the literature. Although Bion's immediate audience of analysts and psychoanalytic psychotherapists has been enriched through the use of containment, which they could grasp sufficiently from his writing to apply in their practice, perhaps there has not been enough to allow the 'ordinary man' to use it. Bion himself wrote about this process, but I am applying it to him as being in the league of 'exceptional people'.

> On this work ordinary men and women with ordinary ability depend to do work that otherwise would be done by only exceptional people. Thanks to Faraday and other scientists ordinary people can illuminate a room by the touch of a switch; thanks to Freud and his co-workers ordinary people hope by psycho-analysis to be able to illuminate the mind. The fact that the world's work has to be done by ordinary people makes this

work of scientification (or vulgarization, or simplification, or communication, or all together) imperative. There are not enough mystics and those that there are must not be wasted.

(Bion, 1970, p. 79)

There are dangers in trying to define and elucidate containment. As has been shown, the concept has already developed through its use in practice, and the danger of a definition is that it then becomes preserved in aspic. Communicating the concept more widely to audiences unfamiliar with the background to the idea means that some of the nuances and depth may be lost. However, the advantages may outweigh these disadvantages if the usefulness of this idea can be recognised and utilised by a wider audience.

Reverie, alpha function and symbolism

I am going to summarise briefly two of Bion's concepts, reverie and alpha function, together with one of Segal's, symbol formation, in order to show how restoring the ability to think is integral to the idea of containment. In the paucity of his writings about containment, Bion still managed to point to some of its ramifications, linking reverie and alpha function to containment to indicate how containment was linked to the ability to think. Segal wrote about how the presence of containment was linked to the development of the ability to symbolise in her later comments (Segal, 1979) on her original paper (Segal, 1957). Symbolic function is also related to the capacity to think. Segal's date of publication of her original paper on the use of symbolism predates Bion's 1959 paper, but she integrated his concept of containment in her 1979 postscript. Alpha function, reverie and symbolic functioning will be explained in more detail below.

In *Learning from Experience*, Bion (1962a) outlines various types of thinking, including the alpha function. His idea of the container had been his first step to providing a mechanism to deal with projection and projective identification. Before this, projective identification was thought of as something that someone did to someone else. The other person was not actively involved in the process, but was a passive receiver of these projections. Containment provided the idea of a container, an active receiver of the communication, which was able to 'contain' it, that is, not be overwhelmed or shattered by it. His next idea, about a type of thinking which he called alpha function, provided a mechanism for this to occur, a mechanism whereby projection and projective identification could be processed. Bion described what the other person could do with projective identification and how they could do it. Williams (1998) refers to this as:

> Bion's description of the vital developmental function of an object that is capable of receiving the projections of feeling and discomforts a child cannot himself give a name to or think about. The containing object receives the projections and attempts . . . to give them a name, modify them and make them thinkable. This Bion referred to as the Alpha function or Reverie, and it can only be performed if the containing object bears the emotional impact of projections and makes 'emotional sense' of them.
>
> (Williams, 1998, p. 95)

In this quotation, Williams could be read as implying that alpha function and reverie are the same. However, although both are involved in the process of containment, they each have a separate function. For instance, alpha function is more active. These differences are described in more detail below. This quotation also emphasises the aspect of the concept of containment where the mother's emotional state becomes changed as she is, to some degree, disturbed by and then processes the emotional communication of the infant.

Bion attempted to classify the elements of thinking via 'the Grid' (Bion, 1962b). Although the Grid is difficult and abstruse and Bion himself was often not very happy with it (Lopez-Corvo, 2003), the ideas represented within it are often referred to in psychoanalytic papers, even if the Grid itself is not often used as an analytic tool. The alpha function, one element in the Grid, refers to the process of thinking by one type of thought. 'Alpha function works over sense experiences and emotions, and if successful, it will produce alpha elements that could be stored as a contact barrier between unconscious and conscious, capable of producing thoughts' (Lopez-Corvo, 2003, p. 27). Bion contrasted alpha-elements with beta-elements, another type of mental element: 'beta-elements are a way of talking about matters which are not thought about at all; alpha elements are a way of talking about elements which, hypothetically, are supposed to be part of thought' (Bion, 1990, p. 41).

Bion referred to reverie in the context of the mother–baby relationship. Hinshelwood defined it as 'a state of calm receptiveness' (1991, p. 420), although the emotional state of the mother is then disturbed as a result of the emotional communication of the infant. It seems to me that reverie is a more preparatory function than alpha function: that is, the mother is in a state of reverie in order to receive the communications and process them by alpha function. Reverie is the state in which the mechanism occurs, a more passive, receptive state of mind. Alpha function is more active and is a process of thinking. In relationship to containment, alpha function is about one thought, whereas containment can be about a multiplicity of thoughts, together with emotion. Reverie is discussed here in the context of containment, but it will be seen later that reverie is also related to an element of the dance of reciprocity.

One aspect of the relationship between containment and thinking is its theoretical link to the development of the capacity to symbolise: symbolic functioning. Segal (1957) wrote about symbol formation and the importance of this capacity within the psychoanalytic process to integrate internal and external experiences.

> The word 'symbol' comes from the Greek term for throwing together, bringing together, integrating. The process of symbol formation is, I think, a continuous process of bringing together and integrating the internal with the external, the subject with the object, and the earlier experiences with the later ones.
>
> (Segal, 1957, p. 171)

Internalising the mother's capacity to think about something creates the internal space, or internal container, in which things can be thought about. The ability to develop symbolic play and use symbolism is part of human life, from art to communication. Symbolic play is one way through which children process their experience. 'Play is of particular value to the child, as it provides possibilities for anxiety-provoking situations to be faced in a symbolical way' (Hoxter, 1977, p. 218). Symbolism is woven through literature, storytelling, art and everyday life. The result of an inability to use symbols can be seen most clearly in autistic children, where everything is concrete and cannot be used to symbolise anything else. For instance, saying, 'That is none of your business' to an autistic adolescent might draw the reply, 'I don't have a business.'

Alpha function, reverie and symbolic functioning are all concepts related to containment. Alpha function and reverie are necessary for containment to take place, while symbolic functioning occurs as a result of containment. All contribute to thinking. The following section will examine the possible organic bases for containment and suggest that, biologically, containment can restore the ability to think.

Organic bases for containment

It may be possible to draw together four bodies of evidence from slightly different research areas that together begin to point to the underlying organic mechanisms for containment. The first is the research on the development of emotional and sensory regulation, the second is the research on the emotional arousal and performance curve, the third is the research on zones of optimal functioning, and the fourth is the research on mirror neurons.

There is now a large body of evidence from many researchers concerning the importance of emotional regulation. Schore (1994) drew together the evidence from biological and neurobiological research and linked this both to child development research and to psychoanalytic concepts to show how emotional regulation develops biologically, yet within a relationship. His book covers an enormous amount of research from disparate disciplines. One quotation which summarises his findings and indicates the range of disciplines he covered is as follows: 'Increasingly complex self-regulatory structural systems mature during infancy, and their development is a product of early dynamic object relational environmental interactions that shape the outcome of genetic predispositions' (Schore, 1994, p. 34). In other words, Schore showed how interaction, from an object relation's perspective, fosters organic development and vice versa. And containment is one of the major mechanisms at the heart of object relations theory.

Through the inter- and intrapersonal mechanism of containment, the infant learns how to manage and process emotions and anxiety. In turn, this leaves him free to develop and use his higher cortical functions of thinking and planning, which, in turn, underlies the development of the infant. Through the experience of being contained, the infant develops an 'internal container', the ability to manage himself. The mechanisms underlying this process are summarised by Schore: 'by providing well modulated socioaffective stimulation, the mother facilitates the growth of connections between cortical limbic and subcortical limbic structures that neurobiologically mediate self-regulatory functions' (Schore, 1994, p. 33). That is, the infant develops connections in the brain in the limbic area, the area of the brain that provides the seat for the emotions, which are then able to regulate emotions and provide the basis for impulse control. The development of these connections in the infant brain is fostered through the 'well modulated' stimulation provided by the principal carer/s. This is consistent with both the concept of containment and that of mutual affect regulation, a 'reciprocity-related' theory.

Emotional regulation and containment also relate to sensory integration. Sensory integration is about being able to regulate the impact of all the information that comes to us through our senses. It is therefore strongly related to the external world. This is linked to emotional regulation, which is more related to both our internal and external worlds. Ayres (1979) looked at how sensory processing and motor planning disorders interfere with daily-life function and learning. The difference is perhaps one of emphasis, in that sensory integration is broadly to do with external stimulation coming in through all of our senses and being able to regulate and integrate the information. Emotional regulation is about information coming in from the external world, but it is also about information generated from our internal world. Containment is involved with both, as it bridges the internal and external worlds. It is about processing emotions, but within a relationship and a communication system. The dance of reciprocity, explained later, also includes the regulation of affect and of incoming sensory stimuli. It is interesting to note that as we progress through an examination of various aspects of containment, links with reciprocity are already becoming manifest: for instance, the link with reverie and the role of reciprocity as well as containment in affect regulation.

Sensory integration is a concept used by occupational therapists in the UK. Jean Ayres, who developed the theory, was an occupational therapist in the USA, but from there it has moved out to other professional groups. In the USA, Greenspan, a psychiatrist, wrote about regulatory disorders when the concept was relatively new (Greenspan, 1993). He distinguished between those children who were having a problem with regulating themselves because their carers had not helped them to develop this capacity and those children who were born with a sensitivity that made it difficult for them to regulate themselves or with a deficiency in their ability to develop this capacity; that is, between those children whose environment had failed to facilitate their development in this area and those children who had an organic reason why they could not regulate themselves. This can be seen as a failure in containment for the first group and for the necessity for more containment for the second group, so that both groups need the experience of containment in order to help them build up their own capacity.

The second body of evidence supporting an organic basis for the functioning of containment comes from psychological research, which has shown that high levels of emotional arousal disrupt the capacity to think (Atkinson et al., 1993), the corollary of which is that decreasing the level of arousal restores the ability to think or perform. I suggest that containment contributes to the processing of emotion and anxiety, reducing arousal and restoring the capacity to think, as the cortical functions in the brain of thinking and planning can then be accessed. This is supported by psychological research on performance and arousal levels. The original papers are over 50 years old. Their findings have been built upon within the discipline of psychology, but have not been applied to psychotherapy theory.

The emotional arousal and performance curve is shaped somewhat like an inverted U, or normal curve, ascending from deep sleep to waking to increasing alertness and an optimal level of performance at the top of the curve, and then descending through increasing emotional disturbance to disorganisation at the bottom of the curve (Hebb, 1949). I think this can be seen to relate to containment restoring the ability to think, that containment is needed because we can become disabled by high levels of emotional arousal. Tyhurst (1951) showed that people differed markedly in their ability to think and function in states of high arousal produced by disaster situations. About 15 per cent of people manage to be organised and effective; most people, about 70 per cent, show some disorganisation, but are still able to be effective; and 15 per cent become so disorganised that they are unable to function. This may be related to people's differing ability to contain themselves, the effectiveness of their 'internal' container. It does show, again, that high levels of arousal disrupt the ability to think and perform. There are stories from the 9/11 disaster of people who were not only able to contain their own emotions and function in that situation, but were also able to help others to contain their terror so that they too could think and act.

Schore (1984) related the biology of arousal ('optimal arousal refers to the maintenance of autonomic balance between sympathetic ergotropic and parasympathetic trophotropic arousals' (Schore, 1984, p. 376)) to emotion ('it is known that moderate levels of arousal . . . are associated with positive affect and focused attention, while extreme levels of arousal . . . are related to negative emotion and distracted attention' (Schore, 1984, p. 376)) and to the carer's role in regulating arousal ('Psychobiologically attuned practicing mothers of securely attached infants maintain the child's arousal within a moderate range that is high enough to maintain interactions (by stimulating the child up out of low arousal states) but not too intense as to cause distress and avoidance (by modulating high arousal states)' (Schore, 1984, p. 376)).

The third area of research suggestive of an organic basis for containment is the zone of optimal functioning (ZOF) research (Hanin,

1980) which developed out of research around the arousal and performance curve, but which looked at the effect of anxiety on athletes' performances. Hanin postulated, on the basis of his research with Russian athletes, that there is a narrow zone of optimal functioning, which is different for everyone. Some athletes performed best when they were relaxed, some performed best when they were very anxious, and some performed best when they were only somewhat anxious. Although this research is in the field of sport psychology, it does not seem a big leap to extrapolate the findings to other types of performance, such as acting or speaking in front of others. A review of ZOF research (Gould & Tuffey, 1996) concluded that generally the research supported the hypothesis. Interestingly, one of their recommendations was that investigation should be made into how athletes developed their particular ZOF. The link to containment is that, in situations where one is competing or performing in front of others, containment provides a mechanism for managing one's anxiety. This does not mean that in containment the emotion or the anxiety has to subside completely in order for the person to think or perform; it means that the anxiety or emotion needs to be at a certain level, or felt to be manageable, and this will be different for all of us and also different at different times. Processing or managing an emotion does not mean that it needs to disappear in order that we can function again. This research may indicate that some people can tolerate, for instance, a higher level of anger, guilt or sadness and still feel that the emotion is manageable and still perform well at, for instance, parenting, lecturing or contributing to a meeting. Further research would be required in order to discover whether athletes were tolerating different levels of anxiety or whether they were processing it differently.

The fourth and final area of research reviewed here which might suggest an organic substrate for containment is that of mirror neurons. There may, of course, be other lines of research. The concept of containment requires that one person can communicate to another how they are feeling, that the other person can communicate back that they have understood and not been overwhelmed, and that the first person can understand this communication. It also includes the idea that the receiver experiences, to some degree, an emotional disturbance, which they are then able to regulate. There is a growing body of work on mirror neurons that may provide some explanation for the understanding of an emotional communication. Mirror neurons in one's own brain seem to be able to fire whether one is carrying out a movement or seeing another carry out a movement. The original work was carried out with monkeys. Keysers et al. (2003) found that with monkeys the same set of neurons fired in the ventral premotor cortex whether the monkey was performing an action or whether the monkey watched or heard another performing the action. Kohler et al. (2002), the same team of researchers, wrote about how others' actions were represented in these mirror neurons. One could postulate that this ability must have evolved because it gave an evolutionary advantage to be able to have some idea of others' intent; that is, to have advanced warning about whether one needed to fight, flee or relate.

This work has been replicated in *Homo sapiens*: while undergoing a brain scan, dancers were shown videos of other dancers dancing, and, again, mirror neurons were found to be firing in their brains (Glaser, 2005).

> Now in the realm of speculation, some people think that your ability to read other people's movement helps you to understand what they are thinking. The way to understand that is that we move differently when we are happy or when we are sad. And, in fact, we can empathise to some extent with the way people are feeling by reading their movements in a special way.
>
> (Glaser, 2005, webpage)

Perhaps mirror neurons give us a subconscious idea of what other people or animals are thinking/feeling. It may be that the work on mirror neurons will provide some detail about how we have trans-ference and counter-transference feelings; that is, how in the therapy the therapists feel that they are being responded to as though they represented someone else for the other person, and how the therapist can have feelings related to the other person's emotions rather than anything to do with the therapist's own self.

The projection of emotion

Projection could be seen as a shorthand psychoanalytic term to describe how emotion is communicated from one person to another, as described by Freud nearly 100 years ago, before the physiological and neurological basis for emotion could begin to be described. Beebe and Lachmann (2002) described and contextualised some studies from 30 years ago, which already advance our knowledge. Ekman (1983) taught actors to reproduce the exact facial movements that result in a particular facial expression. In another task, he taught actors to relive particular emotions. The surprising result was that the group who reproduced the muscle movements also produced the clearer autonomic changes linked to that emotion, such as alteration of heart rate. Beebe and Lachmann concluded that this 'suggests that the physiological state of the receiving partner who matches is very similar to the physiological state of the sending partner' (Beebe & Lachmann, 2002, p. 108).

This chapter has examined the original writings of Bion together with contemporary writings on containment to create a definition of containment, together with the idea that there is a continuum of containment and that the biological basis for it may be beginning to be available in the research literature. The concept has been mainly located within the UK and within the psychoanalytic community, but, hopefully, the fundamental importance of this concept has been illustrated sufficiently to indicate that it deserves wider recognition.

Containment is a concept full of rich texture. It can take a moment to grasp and yet repay years of study. Without the concept, psycho-analytic psychotherapists would not be able to explain many of the infant observations and therapeutic experiences. They would not have the concept available to inform the setting up of therapeutic situations. Other professional groups would not be able to use the concept to inform them how to set up situations and work with other people in a more effective manner (Whitehead & Douglas, 2005; Douglas, 2004a). Without the concept, it would not be possible to focus therapeutic work with mothers and infants to foster better attachments. Its simplicity and profundity and its place at the heart of human relationships have led to its taking its place at the centre of analytic psychotherapy.

4   What is reciprocity?

The origin of the concept

Reciprocity was described by Brazelton in a paper published in 1974 (Brazelton et al., 1974) after he had carried out a frame-by-frame analysis of the filmed interactions between mothers and their babies. He had carried out the filming, however, in 1967 (Trevarthen, 1980), so the results were probably already known to interested child development researchers well before the publication of the 1974 paper. This was the first time that the interaction was minutely recorded within the child development research tradition. Other child development researchers were astonished by the results and have developed various aspects of the idea, which will be described later. The surprise for the scientific community was to see how active and how organised the baby was in relating to its mother. 'I had not realised, at least as a scientist, how expressive and how sensitive a baby could be' (Trevarthen, 1980, p. 317). The baby was not a passive object that simply experienced things happening to it. The baby was active both in eliciting the interaction and in regulating the interaction, from birth. This can be seen in a book (Murray & Andrews, 2000), the first to include extensive frame-by-frame photographs of the interaction between an infant and his mother and father from birth. This, and other subsequent research, has established that a baby is born with far more social skills and acumen than anyone had previously realised.

For simplicity, I am going to refer to the dyad of mother and baby, but this pattern can be seen with any responsive father, grandparent, adult or child.

There are several characteristics of reciprocity. Moments of reciprocity are thought to happen from the very first moments outside the womb between the baby and mother. When all goes well, reciprocal interaction is initiated by both the baby and the mother, using all sensory modalities. It is characterised by rhythm in intense, short bursts, sometimes only for seconds, with pauses between as the baby assimilates the experience. The mother is sensitive to the baby and the baby is sensitive to the mother.

Brazelton et al. (1974) analysed many interactions between infants and their mothers and were able to discern a pattern of interaction, a 'dance', which had recognisable 'steps'. He described a typical inter-action as including seven components: initiation, orientation, state of attention, acceleration, peak of excitement, deceleration, and with-drawal or looking away. Contact is established during *initiation*, the baby turning his face and eyes towards his mother. The baby moves his body and limbs towards her in *orientation* and then, in the *state of attention*, sends and receives cues, using all of his face and body. In *acceleration,* his interaction increases, there are fewer moments of inattention, and he vocalises more, usually starting with bodily activ-ity that leads to a vocalisation. He may smile, spit, move his tongue and cycle with his arms and legs. During the *peak of excitement*, all these behaviours can be present, but he also tries to control the build-up in several ways. 'He may bring his hand to his mouth to suck, suck on his tongue, yawn, or hold onto his hands or onto another part of his body in what appears to be an effort to decrease the building up tension' (Brazelton et al., 1974, p. 57). There is a gradual *deceleration*, followed by *withdrawal*, looking away. Brazelton suggested that this withdrawal is an essential part of the cycle and may be necessary for the baby to process the interaction or regulate the interaction.

One of the cycles of interaction described in Brazelton's paper takes 16 seconds. A great deal of activity occurs within that 16 seconds. However, Trevarthen (2003) has analysed cycles of communication and thinks that, generally, they are more likely to occur in cycles of 30 seconds. He points out that the stanzas of baby songs tend to last 20–30 seconds. He thinks that this may be related to the autonomic cycle, known about for at least 150 years, the time interval the brain uses to regulate the body when at rest. During sleep, heart rate and breathing speed up and slow down within a cycle of 30 seconds. He has carried out research that shows both the rhythm and general musicality of the interaction.

In the final phase of the interaction, that of looking away, Brazelton observed that a baby has two qualitatively different types of withdrawing from an interaction. The first type is a momentary shutting down to decrease inward stimulation while still remaining in contact with the mother. Although the baby is not in direct com-munication with the mother at that point, he is still very aware within the interaction, because he will soon re-engage. The baby probably keeps the mother in peripheral vision. His activity decreases, and his body hardly moves. He may look at something else in a dull fashion, play with his own clothes, smile into the distance, suck on his fingers, or do other activities that serve to decrease his attention on his mother while not providing a real new focus for attention. However, when he is ready, he will quickly become reconnected with the other person. Brazelton suggested that the baby invests energy in maintaining the look-away part of the cycle, just as he invests energy in the interaction part.

> He can use the period of looking away as if he were attempting to reduce the intensity of the interaction, to recover from the excitement it engenders in him, and to digest what he has taken in during the interaction. These perhaps represent a necessary recovery phase in maintaining homeostasis at a time in infancy when constant stimulation without relief could overwhelm the baby's immature systems.
>
> (Brazelton et al., 1974, p. 59)

Current neurobiological research suggests there is another reason for the importance of the look-away step of the dance, which will be detailed later.

The second type of turning away is more intense and purposeful in rejecting the mother or in shutting out the inward stimulation. This occurs when the baby is overwhelmed or finds the situation unpleasant. There are four main strategies the baby uses purposefully to remove the stimulation. The first is by actively withdrawing from it, the second is by rejecting it, the third is by decreasing its power to disturb, and the fourth is by signalling discomfort. The baby actively withdraws by arching away, turning away or shrinking away. The baby rejects the other by pushing the other away with his hands and feet. The baby reduces the other's power to disturb by decreasing his sensitivity to it by falling asleep, yawning or dulling his senses. The baby signals that he has had enough by fussing or crying.

The methods the baby uses either to withdraw slightly or to withdraw more intensely from the interaction have been described in some detail in order to illustrate the wide repertoire of actions a baby is capable of using with intent. And this is only in one part of the cycle. An example of the dance of reciprocity from a book by Stern (1998) illustrates some of the features of reciprocity, again showing how active the baby is in the interaction.

Then Joey's mother moves into a gamelike sequence. She opens her face into an expression of exaggerated surprise, leans all the way forward and touches her nose to his, smiling and making bubbling sounds all the while. Joey explodes with delight but closes his eyes when their noses touch. She then reels back, pauses to increase the suspense and sweeps forward again to touch noses. Her face and voice are even more full of delight and 'pretend' menace. This time Joey is both more tense and excited. His smile freezes. His expression moves back and forth between pleasure and fear.

Joey's mother seems not to have noticed the change in him. After another suspenseful pause she makes a third nose-to-nose approach at an even higher level of hilarity and lets out a rousing 'oooOH!' Joey's face tightens. He closes his eyes and turns his head to one side. His mother realises that she has gone too far and stops her end of the interaction too. At least for a moment she does nothing. Then she whispers to him and breaks into a warm smile. He becomes re-engaged.

(Stern, 1998, p. 57)

The steps of the dance can be seen in this illustration, but it also shows other more general aspects of reciprocity. Although it may seem self-evident, the surprise for the child development researchers who first viewed the filmed interactions was that the interaction involves two active people. For example, Joey's strategy for decreasing the incoming stimuli can be seen. His smile freezes after his mother's second swoop into his face is a bit too overwhelming for him, but she does not notice the change in his facial expression. He then takes more drastic action, both closing his eyes and turning his head away. This time his mother notices that he is shutting down from the interaction, leaves him for a moment to recover and then signals both visually and auditorially, in a quiet and gentle way (thus lowering the temperature of the interaction to match Joey's current need) that she is ready to interact with him again and he joins in with her. One term used in the literature for this aspect of reciprocity is 'rupture and repair' (e.g., Beebe & Stern, 1977; Gianino & Tronick, 1988). This aspect is so important to human interaction that it will be discussed in more detail later.

Reciprocity describes the minutiae which form the basis of communication, relationships and interaction. At times, it involves a rhythm, as with the smiles. It can involve a game: a game involves two people, where each person's actions are related and there are predictable rules. It can be initiated by either person. Sometimes the mother leads; sometimes the baby leads. All babies are different. Some babies need coaxing to join in, some babies are eager to interact. Some babies can even engage a depressed mother. In this example, the mother is available, but it is the baby who initiates the interaction by looking into her eyes. There are examples from infant observations where the infant is even more active in engaging the mother. For instance, Reid (1997) described a seven-month-old infant: 'Freddie arches his back and turns his face towards her. He reaches his little hand up to his mother's cheek and tries for some time to turn her face towards him, but mum seems distracted' (Reid, 1997, p. 68). Besnard (1998) described Maxime's interaction with her when he was one month and two days old, where Maxime is more active than she is.

> I am alone with Maxime. His eyes are wide open, and he looks at me intently. I say hello, adding that he's wide awake now. Maxime seems to appreciate my words, and he smiles broadly at me. Then he starts experimenting with his mouth. He opens it, shuts it again, sucks, clicks his tongue. He is still looking very carefully at me. His body is more restless now; he's moving his arms and legs. He seems very appreciative of the attention I'm giving him. He begins to vocalize, trying out 'aarrhh' sounds, as though directing them at me. He's wriggling about more and more, his vocalizations are coming thick and fast, as though he's trying to tell me a lot of things. I comment on these vocalisations, and Maxime answers me with another flurry of smiles.
>
> (Besnard, 1998, p. 55)

Reciprocal interaction can be verbal, non-verbal or both. It involves all feelings at all levels of intensity, but always within a sense of contact. It involves a regulation of the intensity of feeling between the two people. Tronick developed this aspect of reciprocity (Tronick et al., 1986), which he named mutual affect regulation, pointing out that it was not just the mother involved in the regulation of the feeling, but also the baby. This aspect is related to containment, where the mother regulates the intensity of a feeling so that it is bearable for the baby. However, within the concept of containment, the baby does not regulate the intensity of feeling for the mother. This will be discussed later.

The definition of reciprocity

The definition of reciprocity, generated from the above material, is as follows:

Reciprocity initially describes the sophisticated interactions between a baby and an adult when both are involved in the initiation, regulation and termination of the interaction. Reciprocity applies to the interactions in all relationships.

Rupture and repair

Two aspects of reciprocity have received a great deal of attention from researchers, to such a degree that the activities have been given names. The first is 'rupture and repair' and the second is 'chase and dodge'. The example of Joey, as well as illustrating the dance of reciprocity and a baby's capacity to be active in withdrawing from a situation, also illustrates 'rupture and repair' (Beebe & Stern, 1977; Gianino & Tronick, 1988). This is now a well-documented process whereby a rupture in the synchrony of the relationship is repaired. With Joey, his mother notices that she has overwhelmed him and draws back until he has recovered and wishes to interact with her again. Although it is important to be able to be in step with each other in the dance of reciprocity, it is equally important to be able to get back in step after missing the beat. This is vital in all our relationships, whether with a partner, a child, or a work colleague, or in analysis, because none of us is perfect. Indeed, perfection in the interactive dance would not be helpful to development. There are at least two areas of work based on this premise. An established and growing body of work attests to the importance of rupture and repair for development. This includes an exploration of the idea that rupture and repair is the basis for the development of hope. For instance, Beebe and Lachmann (2002) summarised Tronick's work (Tronick, 1989; Tronick & Gianino, 1986) on rupture and repair as follows: 'The experience of repair increases the infant's effectance, elaborates his coping capacity, and contributes to his expectation of being able to repair that he can bring to other partners' (Beebe & Lachmann, 2002, p. 163) and 'the expectancy is established that repair is possible' (Beebe & Lachmann, 2002, p. 164).

Schore (1994) summarised work by several researchers on the importance of rupture and repair for development. It enables the infant to differentiate and separate himself from his mother (although rupture is not the same as separation), develop self-regulation, tolerate waiting and frustration, and develop further interactional skills. Among others, he quotes Tronick (1989b) that the 'interactive stress of dyadic mismatches allow [sic] for the development of interaction and self-regulatory skills' (Schore, 1994, p. 209).

The experience of being able to repair something or have something repaired may contribute to the ability to have a feeling of hope. In other words, when a rupture occurs within a relationship, the experience is of something going wrong. But, when the rupture is repaired, the experience is of something getting better, improving. Thus, the infant has the experience that situations can improve, which can become the basis for hope and optimism.

Chase and dodge

While 'rupture and repair' as a sequence can broadly be regarded as positive for social and emotional development, 'chase and dodge' is generally viewed as negative. Both researchers and clinicians have described this version of a reciprocal interaction, which Beebe and Stern termed 'chase and dodge' (Beebe & Stern, 1977). In the example of Joey quoted above, Joey 'dodges' his mother, but she quickly realises and withdraws to give him time to calm down before they both re-engage. Chase and dodge occurs when the mother does not pick up the signal that the baby is overwhelmed and needs her to withdraw. Instead she misinterprets the baby's withdrawal and becomes more intrusive or intense in her interaction to try to engage the baby, who then redoubles his efforts to get away, whereupon the mother becomes more intrusive and the situation deteriorates.

In an example described by Beebe and Lachmann (2002), they analysed a film of a sequence of chase and dodge, taken at 24 frames per second, to show the rapid responsiveness between the mother and baby. The baby is very responsive to each movement of the mother, but his actions are all about withdrawal; 'this interaction points to an aspect of early "coping" activity that might perhaps be best characterized as continuous responsivity and vigilance' (Beebe & Lachmann, 2002, p. 114).

If this situation is not corrected, the baby has the experience of rupture in the relationship without the experience of repair. This has several implications for the development of the baby.

Moore (2004) suggests that the infant becomes hyperaroused, as he is not getting help to self-regulate within a reciprocal relationship and he is also becoming hypervigilant. A possible inference from this would be that this process could be involved in conditions related to attention deficit and hyperactivity disorder (ADHD), which will affect his ability to perform, concentrate and sit still at school. Hyperactivity can sometimes be organic, as in ADHD, which is treated with a combination of pharmaceutical drugs and by creating more structure in the environment, but it can also be non-organic, where altering the environment, including interaction with adults, can decrease the hyperarousal (e.g., Winkley, 1996). Hyperaroused children can be extra-sensitive to movement around them; for instance, while at school, they may lash out at a child unexpectedly running past them, with the result of getting into trouble at school. Another possibility is that the baby could become dissociated, cut off from the mother in an effort to 'tune her out'. This may have an impact upon the child's ability to process and manage emotions and situations even when these are not intrusive.

Because the look-away portion of the dance is the section where the baby processes experience both mentally and organically, disruption of this part of the cycle will have an effect not only on the internalisation of relationships, but also on the development of the brain. The development of the brain is experience dependent (Kotulak, 1993). Most brain development occurs within the first three years of life. Brain development occurs within the context of relationships (Schore, 2001). The presence or absence of the optimal level of stimulation can result in the child having 25 per cent more or 25 per cent fewer connections in his brain (Perry, 1995), and this will affect his response to other people and therefore his future life. The lack of a positive reciprocal relationship may affect the infant's response to other people. However, if the baby has a substantial amount of experience of a sensitive reciprocal relationship with someone else, such as a grandmother or father, this can offset the poor experience with his mother (Crockenburg et al., 1993).

In my opinion, reciprocity is one of the major processes contributing to the development of the quality of attachment (together with containment), as will be commented upon in more detail later.

Some mothers who become caught up in chase and dodge interactions are those with low self-esteem. They may be teenage mothers or mothers with postnatal depression. Anecdotal accounts from my local Sure Start centre, where the information about the cycle of reciprocity, including the look-away section, is shared with the mothers, is that this information can have an immediate positive effect on the mother–baby interaction. The mother ceases to interpret the baby's actions as a personal rejection and therefore ceases to chase the baby in order to get him to interact with her to prove that he does like her. She can see the turning away as a necessary part of the baby's development and as a part of the baby's usual interaction with everybody.

Reciprocity and joy

Reciprocity is involved with emotions such as joy and pleasure. Containment is usually associated with the more 'difficult' emotions, such as anger, sadness, fear, guilt and envy, although, personally, I think that containment is also about processing positive emotions. It is just that, because containment has been written about by clinicians using clinical situations, which by their nature are about difficulties and pathology, the development of theory has concentrated on these more troublesome emotions. Reciprocity, however, has been written about by child development researchers concentrating on normal child development as well as abnormal development. I think this has left them the option of considering more positive emotions. Stern (1990) implied that the capacity for joy grows within a relationship, that is, a reciprocal relationship.

> Joy is the product of a mutual regulation of social exchange by both partners. Smiling back and forth is the prototypical example; it usually begins at a relatively low level of intensity. Each partner then progressively escalates – kicking the other into higher orbit, so to speak. The exchange occurs in overlapping waves, where the mother's smile elicits the infant's, reanimating her next smile at an even higher level, and so on. These over-lapping waves build in intensity, until, most often, simultaneous mutual hilarity breaks out.
>
> (Stern, 1990, p. 16)

Freud began his career by working on the organic basis of the nervous system, and if he were alive today, he would no doubt be fascinated by the progress in neurobiological research. With the state of knowledge available to him in the early 1900s, he thought that unpleasure corresponded to an increase in stimulation or excitation, and pleasure corresponded to a decrease in excitation, the constancy principle (Freud, 1920/1991). Schore (1994) stated that current research shows that joy or pleasure is mediated through an increase in the activity of a circuit (the ventral tegmental dopaminergic system if you want to find out more!), not by a decrease in activity. He suggested that this supports object relations theory, in that the infant is generally motivated by seeking objects, that is, relationships with objects, not by seeking a decrease in excitation. He summarised the large body of research available by 1994 to show how reciprocal interactions underlie the development of emotions, which are in turn supported by the development of the organic substrate in the central nervous system and the limbic system.

Reciprocity and evolution

Presumably, reciprocity has been involved in both shaping and being shaped by our evolution. Those who watch animal observation programmes on the television will know that animals who live in social networks have bigger brains with more connections than solitary animals, in order to cope with the complexity of social relationships. Human beings have evolved as a social species where reciprocity is essential in learning how to relate to other people in a culture. Some form of reciprocity must also be vital for most mammals, where the baby is dependent on the mother for a considerable length of time. It may be that reciprocity is nearly as fundamental as the instinct to feed. Maslow's hierarchy (Maslow, 1970) suggests that feeding is a more basic instinct, necessary for physical survival. However, after this, social communication (which the feeding experience is a part of) is also vital for the development of the child. Indeed, reciprocity is woven through all our fulfilment of needs. Some level of attunement is required to know when a baby is hungry or thirsty, or when the baby is ready to move through a developmental stage, such as weaning or toilet training. Any observation of a mother feeding a baby shows the importance of reciprocity in feeding. At a macrolevel, the mother needs to know when the baby is ready to feed or stop feeding, or when the baby is ready to be weaned. At a microlevel, the way in which the mother offers the breast or bottle to the baby; her adjustment to the baby's needs, to the baby's rhythm of suck and pause; the baby's adjusting to the mother; and the communication between them are all part of reciprocity. Later the rhythm of spoon-feeding is an intricate negotiation between the feeder and the fed.

Attunement, affect regulation and intersubjectivity

So far, we have considered various aspects of reciprocity itself. However, once the idea of reciprocity was established in 1974, there was an explosion of related theoretical terms between 1974 and 1986. These are reciprocity-related theories: attunement (Stern, 1985), mutual affect regulation (Tronick et al., 1986) and intersubjectivity (Trevarthen, 1980). It is interesting that this echoes the establishment of 'containment' and related theoretical terms. The naming of something makes the concept available for further exploration by others.

There is presumably a relationship between the degree to which the concept is felt to be important and the number and breadth of the subsequent developments of the idea.

Reciprocity is one of the major theories in child development research. It has inspired a great number of research studies looking into different aspects of reciprocity and generating further questions, from the general to the particular. For example, Beatrice Beebe has looked at macro-issues, such as how reciprocity contributes to the origins of self and object representations (Beebe & Lachmann, 1988) and has also focused on micro-issues, such as how rhythm, in particular vocal rhythm, contributes to reciprocity (Beebe et al., 2000) and attachment (Beebe & Lachmann, 2002).

Stern's concept of *attunement* emphasised the internal emotional aspect of reciprocity. There are several steps on the path to attunement. The parent interprets the baby's emotional state from the baby's behaviour. The parent performs a behaviour back to the baby that corresponds in some way to the baby's emotional state, so as to convey emotional resonance to the baby (Stern emphasised that this was not the same as imitation, as imitation occurs initially in the same modality between the mother and baby). The baby understands that the parent's response is related to the baby's emotional state.

Parents tend to respond through imitation in the same mode with young infants, but later shift to responding cross-modally. That is, they respond in a different modality from the one currently being used by the infant. This is shown in the following example:

> A nine-month-old boy bangs his hand on a soft toy, at first in some anger but gradually with pleasure, exuberance and humour. He sets up a steady rhythm. Mother falls into his rhythm and says, 'kaaaaa-bam, kaaaaa-bam,' the 'bam' falling on the stroke and the 'kaaaaa' riding with the preparatory upswing and the suspenseful holding of his arm aloft before it falls.
>
> (Stern, 1995, p. 140)

The boy is expressing himself by using the movement of his hand and arm. The mother is expressing herself by using her verbal facility.

The parent does not match the baby's behaviour, but the emotional state is associated with that behaviour. 'Affect attunement, then, is the performance of behaviours that express the quality of feeling of a shared affect state without imitating the exact behavioural expression of the inner state' (Stern, 1995, p. 142).

These experiences of sharing an emotion are important, because it is within these interactions that the infant learns about emotional states.

> Interpersonal communication, as created by attunement, promotes infants coming to recognise shared internal feeling states and the rules of social discourse. The converse is also true; feeling states that are never attuned will not become part of the infant's developing repertoire.
>
> (Seifer & Dickstein, 2000, p. 155)

The main aspect of reciprocity that Stern's concept developed was the idea of cross-modal communication. Although parents and infants imitate each other within the same modality, he and subsequent researchers, such as Beebe, have described in detail how parents and adults often match and expand the infant's communication within another modality. Knowing this can lead to extensions in technique when working with mothers and infants who are currently in a relationship characterised by low reciprocity (e.g., Beebe & Lachmann, 2002).

However, Stern's emphasis is on the role of the parent and how this affects the communication within the dyad. One of the main revelations of reciprocity was to show how both the parent and the infant are active in the relationship; that a baby is born predisposed to communicate. Stern's concept shares with containment, rather than reciprocity, the emphasis on the role of the parent.

In Stern's concept of attunement, the emphasis is on the parent matching the emotional state of the child. In Tronick's concept of *mutual affect regulation*, the clue lies in the word 'mutual'. The baby is as much in control of the social interaction as the parent. The baby acts to control the social interaction by giving out emotional signals, to try to get the parent to act reciprocally. If this happens, the baby has an experience of being effective. If this does not happen, the baby has an experience of being helpless. The parent is also involved in this process, and the baby's success or failure will also depend on the sensitivity and cooperation of the parent. The members of the dyad are thus interdependent. Tronick includes the element of rupture and repair in his concept, in that, if there is a rupture in the interaction, then the baby also has another chance to try again, and if it works, the baby has a renewed sense of effectiveness: 'Positive development may be associated with the experience of coordinated interactions characterized by frequent reparations of interactive errors and the transformation of negative affect into positive affect' (Tronick, 1989, p. 112). Tronick found that mutually coordinated interaction between the baby and mother was found about 30 per cent of the time. Switches between coordinated and uncoordinated states occurred rapidly, approximately every three to five seconds.

Stern emphasises the development in the infant of the recognition of emotions through affect attunement. Tronick emphasises the development of the regulation of emotion and arousal states and of the development of a sense of effectiveness in the infant. His work has led to further research on the regulation of emotion and how this is affected when the adult is 'absent in mind', whether through depression (Tronick & Weinberg, 1997), mental illness, or substance abuse (Lester & Tronick, 1994). Crockenburg and Leerkes (2000) describe further studies which have emanated from Tronick's idea.

The knowledge about regulation of emotion has consequences for the work of Youth Offending Teams and those involved with the precursors of offending behaviour within other UK government programmes such as On Track. Not being able to regulate emotion, arousal levels and impulses can lead to offending behaviour (Karr-Morse & Wiley, 1997). Current government initiatives focus on earlier and earlier intervention as the early genesis of offending behaviour is increasingly recognised.

Trevarthen called his concept *'intersubjectivity'*. In an early paper, he wrote:

> Infants a few months old make speech-like patterns of movement when they are also clearly overcome by some rudimentary purpose to influence, impress, or lead the attentions they have obtained of another. Even though no meaningful information about the world is transmitted, the act is clearly one of psychological communication that may be said to show 'intersubjectivity' . . . remind[ing] one of the interplaying melodies of music.
>
> (Trevarthen, 1974, p. 72)

He later used Mary Bateson's term of 'proto-conversations' (Bateson, 1971) for these early conversations that did not involve words from the baby, but where the baby used all its body to communicate as well as using sounds. Hand gestures and leg movements were all part of the communication, as shown in Brazelton's film (Brazelton et al., 1974). Trevarthen also developed his interest in the link between this proto-conversation and music.

Trevarthen used the term 'subjectivity' to refer to 'the totality of the baby's rudimentary powers to use external objects to satisfy perception exploration, manual prehension and the like . . . the condition of being a coordinated subject, motivated to act with purpose to the outside world' (Trevarthen, 1980, p. 324). In other words, 'subjectivity' refers to the baby's interaction with things, and 'intersubjectivity' refers to the baby's two-way interaction with people.

Trevarthen (1980) outlined seven motives which he thought underlay intersubjectivity. I have categorised each of the seven motives, from a biological motive, through a social motive to a motive for the achievement of mastery, in order to highlight the aim of the expressed behaviours. The first I have categorised as biological: to coordinate with feeding and cleaning and to get mother's attention by expressing alarm, hunger or pain. The second is attachment related: to seek proximity and to watch both verbal and non-verbal signals and become engaged in the process. The third is linked to language: to respond with pleasure and to use prespeech movements of lips, tongue, and hands and preverbal vocalisations. The fourth is emotion related: to exhibit emotions, intent and pleasure in mastery. The fifth is social: to engage in reciprocal interaction, which includes the emotional state of the other and where each adjusts to the other. The sixth is biological, social and emotional: to express distress in the face of threat by another and confusion if the other's actions cannot be understood. The seventh is related to mastery: 'to avoid excessive, insensitive, or unwanted attempts by others to communicate, thus to retain a measure of personal control over one's state of expression to others' (Trevarthen, 1980, p. 327).

Trevarthen outlined a stage of secondary intersubjectivity, starting around the age of nine months, when he thought that the infant began to learn by example from the mother. The baby is able to move from a dyadic to a triadic relationship, including a third object. For instance, the baby can become interested in his mother's interest in his toy, so a third object is included. This links to the psychoanalytic theory of the Oedipal position, where the baby sees his mother talking to his father. Trevarthen seems to have moved to study the earlier rather than the later stages of development, as he is now using video material from babies who are only a few weeks old (e.g., Trevarthen, 2003) and is moving to study premature babies, who 'have very elaborate hand movements which have never been studied' (Trevarthen, 2003, p. 71) and 'do not show their communicative talents unless they are in an intimate contact with a sympathetic human being' (Trevarthen, 2003, p. 71).

Trevarthen (2003) analysed proto-conversations together with a musician. He found similar patternings within the proto-conversation to those Brazelton had found in analysing verbal and non-verbal behaviour. Trevarthen used the musical terms of introduction, development, climax and resolution instead of Brazelton's named stages of initiation, orientation, state of attention, acceleration, peak of excitement, deceleration, and withdrawal, looking away.

Attunement, affect regulation and intersubjectivity have all been developed since the description of reciprocity, each researcher developing their idea out of Brazelton's analysis of the filmed interactions. Thus, all these concepts are related, but each has a different emphasis. For instance, Seifer and Dickstein (2000) considered the relationship between attunement and mutual affect regulation. They thought that both used the idea that the baby's emotions were used to coordinate social communication. However, the difference between them was that in attunement the parent matches the baby's inner emotional state, so that the parent is much more active than the baby. In affect regulation, the baby is as active as the parent in controlling the social exchange.

Stern is perhaps closest to the concept of containment, with the idea that the parent is more active in engaging with the baby and in giving meaning to the baby's communication. Stern emphasises the role of the parent in helping the baby to develop a sense of self and highlights the role of cross-modal communication.

Tronick emphasises the importance of two-way communication for the regulation of emotion, which has substantial implications for the future of the baby in terms of its ability to participate in relationships and society. Tronick has developed an interest in the consequences for the baby if the mother's ability to participate in affect regulation is compromised by her mental illness. This then extrapolates to other situations where the mother's capacity to interact sensitively is compromised, as where the mother is often under the influence of drugs or alcohol. 'Of particular concern in considering women who have used drugs during pregnancy is their ability to develop interactions with their infant' (Lester et al., 2000, p. 166). Here, Lester, building on the work of Tronick (e.g., Lester & Tronick, 1994), is emphasising the central importance of the relationship, as well as the care-taking ability of the parent.

Tronick has provided the catalyst for the work on the importance of rupture and repair in human life. Mutual affect regulation is also linked to containment. Although Tronick emphasises the role of the baby as well as that of the mother in affect regulation, whereas containment emphasises the role of the mother, mutual affect regulation is linked to containment because it is about the process within the dyad that enables the baby to learn how to process and manage emotional states. This will be discussed in more detail later.

Trevarthen emphasises the role of the motivation of the baby in the two-way communication between the mother and baby. He highlights the role of rhythm and musicality in interactions (e.g., Trevarthen, 1999).

It is interesting to explore the link between intersubjectivity and object relations theory, that is, between a reciprocity-related child development concept and psychodynamic theory. Braten (1987), in considering intersubjectivity, put forward a mechanism that is similar to that of Bion's preconception mating with the realisation to create a conception. Braten (1987) proposed that babies are born with circuits within their central nervous system that specify the presence of a 'virtual other', the potential presence of a complementary participant. The actual other is realised by the other person's becoming present in the relationship with the baby. If technology ever allows these postulated circuits to be found, it would be an organic confirmation of Bion's theory. Braten focused on the relationship, using a systems theory perspective to suggest that the system is the pattern for a single organisation between the mother and baby, that is, the relationship, rather than the two separate systems of two separate people. Although there is obviously a baby and a mother, two people, the idea of the importance of the relationship is borne out by Winnicott's famous remark that there is no such thing as a baby (Winnicott, 1965). However, this appears to be another case where the paradigm of both/and is more helpful than either/or. The mother and baby are in a relationship that could be looked at as one system, but they are also two individual systems who are also in relationship to others, to their environment and to their own inner world.

The seeds of most of the work on reciprocity-related concepts can be seen in Brazelton's original paper. He wrote about the rhythm in the interaction, the two-way nature of reciprocity, the intentional nature of the baby's communication, the emotional aspect, the regulatory aspect and the importance of the look-away cycle. Different child development researchers are developing different aspects of the idea and are increasingly looking at younger and younger babies, from premature babies to those still developing in the womb (e.g., Campbell, 2004).

Organic bases for reciprocity

Just as different avenues of research are suggesting possible organic substrates for containment, so there are also possible organic bases for reciprocity. Schore suggested that in these affectively synchronized, psychobiologically attuned face-to-face interactions, the infant's right hemisphere, which is dominant for the infant's recognition of the maternal face, and for the perception of arousal-inducing maternal facial affective expressions, visual emotional information, and the prosody of the mother's voice, is focusing her attention on and is, therefore, regulated by the output of the mother's right hemisphere, which is dominant for nonverbal communication, the processing and expression of facially and prosodically expressed emotional information, and for the maternal ability to comfort the infant.

(Schore, 2003, p. 18)

Ryan et al. (1997) used electroencephalography (EEG) and neuroimaging data to show that 'the positive emotional exchange resulting from autonomy-supportive parenting involves participation of right hemispheric cortical and subcortical systems that participate in global, tonic emotional modulation' (Ryan et al., 1997, p. 719).

In other words, the accumulation of data from many research studies suggests that the right brain is the dominant hemisphere for tuning into another's emotions, by processing both visual and auditory data. (It would be interesting to know more about how mirror neurons fit into this process.) The left brain is more involved with construing verbal data. At birth, the right brain of the baby is already more developed than the left brain (Schore, 1994), and the communication between the right brain of the mother and the right brain of the baby means that the mother will be helping the further development of the right brain functions. This is important because it is the right brain that regulates the hormones and physiology related to emotion and impulse control.

The baby already has some innate social ability at birth, as clearly demonstrated in the frame-by-frame photographs of Murray and Andrews (2000), presumably mediated through the more advanced development of the right hemisphere of the brain at birth. The second-by-second interaction between the baby and his mother builds up the synaptic connections in the brain, which then form the basis for reciprocity-linked development, such as language, emotional regulation, attachment and interpersonal relationships. Both nature and nurture are therefore involved in reciprocity. Trevarthen (2003) pointed out that when babies are having a proto-conversation (the precursor of a conversation with words) with their mothers, they tend to use their right arm more than their left. He suggested that this is linked to the development of the left brain, in that the right side is controlled by the left brain, which is also the speech and language centre, so that as the desire to communicate is expressed with the right arm, so the left hemisphere is being stimulated, preparing the way for the development of language.

Although the whole dance of reciprocity is involved in developing the synaptic connections in the brain, there is evidence that the look-away section has a particular role to play. Brazelton had already intimated in his original paper (Brazelton et al., 1974) that he thought that the look-away cycle served to reduce the intensity of the inter-action in order to give the infant a quieter space in which to process the preceding interaction, as mentioned earlier. This has been sup-ported by data from studies on baby brain development, in that synapse formation is at its zenith in the look-away or withdrawal cycle (Moore, 2004; Perry, 1995; Schore 1994, 1996, 2001).

There has been some interesting research on gaze aversion in children.

> There is a tendency in many cultures to encourage children to 'look at me while I'm speaking to you', and to interpret looking away as a sign of disengagement or lack of interest. What our research clearly showed was that primary-school-aged children used gaze aversion to help them concentrate on difficult material. Therefore, provided the aversion is appropriately timed within the interaction (i.e. especially during thinking, and to a lesser extent during speaking), it is something to be encouraged rather than discouraged.
>
> (Doherty-Sneddon, 2004, p. 82)

I think that there is a link to reciprocity and neurological processing, with the need to time looking away within the context of a reciprocal interaction and that neurological processing appears to occur within the look-away cycle. However, the author of the above paper seems unaware of the research on reciprocity.

Neurological research is providing data to show how the biology of the brain lends credence to the view that, firstly, infants are prepared from birth and even before birth to interact with others and, secondly, that infants develop emotionally and socially within the context of the relationship. The organic substrates are beginning to be outlined that support the ideas on reciprocity and containment. Knowledge of the functions of the primitive brain, limbic brain and cortex perhaps point to more of our unconscious material lying in the primitive brain and limbic brain, while the cortex is involved in more conscious thinking and processing.

Why didn't psychotherapists notice?

The observation of infants and children has been part of the psychoanalytic tradition since the days of Freud, as psychoanalysts tried to understand the development and mechanisms of the mind. This tradition was augmented by Esther Bick, who instituted the observation of infants as a specific learning experience (Bick, 1964), predating the publication of Brazelton's results by ten years. The question then arises why none of these observers approached the development of a reciprocity-like concept. Although the experience of closely observing infants did illustrate how active infants were in construing their world, the emphasis for the theoretical developments arising from the observations was perhaps more on observing how the infant dealt with mental experience than on focusing on the actual relationship between the mother and baby. Observed interaction between the baby and another was seen through the lens of containment and other psychoanalytic ideas. Psychoanalysts were more interested in looking at how the baby developed internal, intrapsychic mechanisms than in how the baby interacted with its caregivers. The focus was more internal than external.

Perhaps because there was already a lot to say about this internal world of the infant, the eyes of psychoanalytic psychotherapists were not focused on the external relationships, even though containment requires the presence of another to begin the process. It was also a theoretical given within psychoanalytic writings that the mother provided the container for the baby; the baby did not provide a container for the adult. The baby's ability to contain its own feelings developed very slowly through the experience of being contained by the mother. Within the psychoanalytic tradition, there are many names for interpsychic phenomena: transference, counter-transference, projection, projective identification and containment. But these are described in terms relating to the individual's developing internal mental mechanisms, not as something related to the development of external relationships with people. This may be for two reasons.

Firstly, psychoanalysis has from its inception looked at how individuals manage their internal mental phenomena. Analysis was set up with that in mind. Indeed, the relationship between the analyst and analysand was seen as an interference in this process. As Freud became aware of transference, he first tried to avoid it, before examining it and incorporating it into the body of psychoanalytic ideas. The same happened with counter-transference, until Paula Heimann committed her thoughts about it to paper in 1950. The relationship component of the analysis, between the analyst and analysand, i.e. the interaction, was not a focus in and of itself. It was only used in the service of illustrating and developing the internal psychic structures of the individual.

Secondly, during the 1970s and 1980s, when reciprocity and its related concepts were being developed, the dispute between Bowlby (who created attachment theory) and the Kleinians was in full swing. At that time, Kleinian practice was to concentrate more on the internal world of the patient, possibly sometimes to the detriment of the external world. Hegel's ideas have already been outlined earlier, so one could perhaps predict that an antithesis was produced in reaction to this thesis, and, indeed, Bowlby took up the position of emphasising the external world. Both sides took up increasingly polarised positions (with correspondingly frosty relations with each other) until the move towards a synthesis began in the 1990s, and is still continuing today (cf. Fonagy, 2001). Because the focus of the psychoanalytic psychotherapists was on the internal world, even though they must have seen the dance of reciprocity many times, they did not name it. I am suggesting, however, that this process of reciprocity occurs in the therapy room and would repay some attention.

Why did Brazelton notice reciprocity? Other child development researchers were doing experiments with mothers and infants and must have seen the dance of reciprocity, but, like the psychoanalysts, they did not name it. I would conjecture that Brazelton's interest in the interaction also came from 'learning by doing' in his clinical practice, in that he was a paediatrician who saw many infant–mother dyads. In the introduction to his paper, he wrote that he had always been interested in (and had noticed) the rhythmical interactions between babies and their mothers. He had also noticed that 'initial synchrony ended in dyssynchrony after a difficult or tense interaction' (Brazelton et al., 1974, p. 49). This had led to his proposing the use of film analysis to take a closer look at the interaction.

5   Can reciprocity be seen in psychotherapy sessions with children?

This chapter begins with a look at the origins of my observations of reciprocity in my psychoanalytic psychotherapeutic clinical material and then progresses to an examination of the description by others of their clinical sessions to see whether it is possible to discern examples of reciprocity occurring even when the clinician has little knowledge of the concept. I first reported the details of Kylie's sessions in an earlier article (Douglas, 2002).

Kylie

During my work with Kylie, introduced in Chapter 1, I was using my understanding of the transference and counter-transference relationship to make interpretations (Joseph, 1985; Symington, 1986), that is, putting into words her reactions to me and the feelings she engendered in me. This is the bread and butter of therapeutic work, but it often felt to me that I was sending these interpretations out into the ether, rather than that they were connecting with another person.

However, indications were that they were beginning to make a difference, because Kylie's play would shift, moving on from one theme to another, and she slowly progressed to a more successful use of splitting. Splitting occurs when a child is able to keep the bad things separate from the good things (Freud, 1940/1991; Klein, 1946/1988), that is, is able to maintain two separate points of view. There is a stage before splitting where the child has been able to build up a good object as well as a bad object, so that the two can then be kept separate. For instance, a child who is angry with his mother says, 'I hate you', but is also able to keep in mind that he loves her. Hinshelwood (1991) gives the example of 'the child who believes in Father Christmas, and has all the excitement and appropriate response on Christmas night even though he has learned the reality that it is "only Dad dressed up"'.

Disturbed children cannot keep separate, for example, their loving feelings and their hating feelings about the same person. This has severe effects on their psychological functioning, because, on an emotional and a physical level, they can feel that everything becomes contaminated (hence Kylie's need to wash her hands and change her clothes). As I look back on my work with Kylie, which included reviewing my notes, it seemed that there was a turning point in our relationship when she was able to split, having built up a good object. When she was able to keep me sometimes as a good object in her mind, it became possible to talk to her in more of a collaborative way, using interpretations of her play and interactions with me. As soon as she established this ability, she immediately initiated a sequence of reciprocal interaction.

The first example of successful splitting occurred in the second term of our work together, when Kylie was almost four years of age.

> First, she told me she was Miss Honey and I was Mrs Trunchball (these are characters from Roald Dahl's story of Matilda. The names speak for themselves!). She held the baby doll, carrying her in the crook of her arm, saying that she wants to feed the baby and almost looking as if she is about to put the baby to the breast (Miss Honey). She walks over to the bin and for a second suspends the baby doll upside down over the bin (Mrs Trunchball), before bringing her back up, saying she is Miss Honey and taking the baby over to the table, where the baby sits on Kylie's lap in front of the plate. Kylie tries to feed her, giving the impression of being rough at times, but trying to keep things under control.
>
> (Douglas, 2002, p. 30)

Here, successful splitting had allowed there to be a good object who can feed the baby. She had split us into the good one (Miss Honey) and the bad one (Mrs Trunchball). In this segment, the fact that she was able to keep the play scene under control was quite an achievement, as often her play would disintegrate into chaos. It is difficult to convey the depth of her anxiety at these times, when she could, literally, become disabled by it, becoming incoherent and uncoordinated. In this segment, she was able to keep the good separate from and therefore safe from being contaminated by the bad.

It may be that splitting is a necessary precondition for reciprocity. The impulse to reach out and have live interaction with such an external object perhaps occurs, using Bion's terms, only when the preconception of a good responsive object is met by a concept to produce a realisation. That is, the child participates in a reciprocal interaction when he recognises the good object.

Immediately following this, Kylie initiated a sequence of reciprocal interactions.

> She starts singing, picking up the toy blue wooden settee and using it as a pipe/mouth organ. She instructs me to clap, looking pleased as I follow her rhythm. I wonder if this is what music therapy is. She takes the settee out of her mouth and goes over to the wall, using it to mark the wall, then comes back and sits down asking me to sing 'Twinkle, twinkle, little star' to her. I do so and she looks pleased again. When I finish she starts to sing 'The wheels on the bus go round, round, round' wanting me to do the actions, which she shows me when we get to ones I don't know. I have the feeling that this session we are managing to do things together.
>
> (Douglas, 2002, p. 31)

For the first time in the sessions, there was a feeling of togetherness. This feeling was also quite direct and intense. I think that it was this point that was pivotal in the establishment of a responsive maternal object. I had become 'live company' (Alvarez, 1992). Both Brazelton and Trevarthen emphasise the importance of rhythm in reciprocal interactions, while Trevarthen, as mentioned previously, also writes about the importance of musicality in reciprocity, nursery songs being in the same 20–30-second time frame as the dance of reciprocity.

The establishment of me as a responsive object led to the feeling in the room that we were two people working together. This was a sign of progress, because, rather than the sessions feeling like two separate people in the room who were not communicating with each other, it now felt as if we were a reciprocal dyad, or two people interacting.

This feeling accelerated over one week into the presentation of an Oedipal situation; that is, that we could progress from being two people together, to tolerating the idea of there being a third person too. This is seen as a sign of progress in therapy, because it allows the child to tolerate the idea of having two parents and to work with her feelings that they have a relationship with each other that sometimes does not include the child. Four sessions later, in the week after the singing session that had created the feeling of us as an interactive couple, she drew a picture of her mother, her father and herself. By the end of the session, she drew another picture where she interposed herself between her mother and her father, and this allowed us to work through her Oedipal feelings.

At the same time as an external responsive object became more evident, it also became clearer when it was disappointing. That is, as she saw and experienced me more as a responsive person who was, at times, in tune with her, she also noticed much more keenly when I was not in tune with her. When, inevitably, there was a rupture in our reciprocal relationship, she would feel the disappointment very intensely. An 'ordinary' repair of altering my interaction to get back in tune with her was not enough. When I was disappointing, she would disintegrate until I could talk to her directly about what she felt. For example, if I was unable to follow her play so that my interpretations were wrong, she would turn the room into a big mess, or suddenly become clumsy and fall or trip. I then had to repair the interaction by describing what had just happened and her disappointment in me. However, I noticed that I was now able to address her more directly about what I felt had happened and that she was developing more of a capacity to take in what I said, so that our interaction was repaired more quickly.

Reciprocity was also involved in later work, in building up sequences of interpretations. Although this was not the second-to-second dance of reciprocity, it was reciprocity in the sense of the rhythm of the to and fro of an interaction, as referred to in Brazelton's original paper (Brazelton et al., 1974) and in the subsequent work of Trevarthen (e.g., Trevarthen, 1999). Before this, it seemed that she was only able to take in a short sentence about one thing from me. The usual sequence of reciprocity where one builds on the other, working together through a cycle, was usually absent in our sessions, and that was why the session in which we worked on a song together was so memorable. However, after another year and a half of work after the 'singing session', we were able to work together in a reciprocal interaction, where she acted out and told me elements of a story that I put together, she waiting for me to finish and I waiting for her, as we built up the story.

> She told me that she had the shop, I had no money. As I elaborated on this, as the one with nothing whilst she had everything, she developed the story and we got into a *rhythm*. I was old, with no money, then I wanted something to eat, but the other children had all the food, there was nothing for me, then I couldn't wait, I wanted everything right now, then I was spiteful, then I was sad, then I was pestering all the time, I wanted one toy, then the other children had them all, then I wanted all the toys.

She got the mattress cushion out and tied it up to the blinds cord. This became a very desirable yummy object that I wanted and I wanted it right now. I spoke about how hard all this was, having to wait, feeling spiteful, wanting something and feeling that other children had it all, there was none for me.

(Douglas, 2002, p. 31)

The development of reciprocity is indicated by the feeling of rhythm in the session, together with our ability to build up the story together. This long and clear sequence would not have been possible early in the therapy. Earlier we would only be able to make explicit one or two parts, fragments of what was now a whole sequence of interactions. Now we could make these feelings explicit together, building on each other's contribution and linking up a sequence. There was also a major element of containment present, in that I had to be the container for all the feelings. I was to have and to hold the feelings of desperation.

In thinking about our work together, I began to think that for Kylie's particular situation it was helpful to think about reciprocity as well as containment. Engaging together in an interactive relationship that had the quality of interacting with very young children seemed to be helpful to her. It seemed that this allowed us then to think about her anxieties and work on containing them. With her, it felt that I had to establish a responsive object before I could establish a containing object. For other very distressed children, perhaps a containing object needs to be established before reciprocity can occur. I was interested to see whether this experience of reciprocity occurred in other therapists' work, and I wondered how it related to containment, which was the familiar concept that we all worked with.

Sula, Michael, Robbie, Sean, Georgie, Helen, Tim, Freddie and Maxime

The phenomenon of reciprocity occurs in the earliest of interactions with a baby and is often intense and momentary, but leads to a heightened feeling of being in touch with each other. The following examples drawn from therapists' publications of their work illustrate various aspects of their experience of a reciprocal interaction, even though they were, in the main, unaware of the concept.

Louise Emanuel (1997) described an instance with a very deprived little girl. Sula, aged six years, was brain damaged from oxygen deprivation during birth and showed autistic features. She had a depressed mother and was on the Child Protection Register for being at risk of physical neglect.

> At one point she banged the scissors on the table and it made a refreshing metallic sound. I took the scissors and tapped them on the table near her, and then put my hand on the table and she tapped near it; finally she gently patted my hand and our eyes met briefly. I said, 'There is someone else here, interested in something different about Sula.' I felt that we had made some wholesome contact.
>
> (Emanuel, 1997, p. 286)

Emanuel described how Sula made rapid progress within a year and divided the therapy sessions into three phases. She characterised the first phase as filtering and amplifying.

> The room suddenly seemed too bright, too over-full of objects. She was like a little baby exposed to too many new sensations at once and her writhing movements and rolling head seemed to be an attempt to shut out the intensity of the experience, as infants often do when intruded upon by too many stimuli. What followed seemed like a dance between us composed of minute steps and movements.
>
> (Emanuel, 1997, p. 290)

Also in this phase of therapy, Emanuel described how 'I found myself being far more active than I am normally and Sula responded, delighted when I rolled a toy car back to her, then amplified her shouts by making them into car noises' (Emanuel, 1997, p. 291). Again in this phase the following occurred.

> She bit off a piece of her rubber and began chewing it. My usual comments about the wrong stuff going into her mouth were not heard and I began to worry that she could swallow it and choke. I opened her mouth, got it out and undeterred she placed it in her mouth again! This battle for control continued for some time and I persisted in stopping her from chewing it. Suddenly she stopped . . . she looked quite different, more beautiful and had a real intelligence in her eyes.
>
> (Emanuel, 1997, p. 293)

Emanuel thought that stopping Sula from swallowing the rubber was a containing experience, together with an incident where she surprised herself by physically reaching out to the girl to hold her arms to stop her picking off her skin. However, I think that the other incidents described in this account are examples of reciprocity and cannot be explained by the concept of containment. Reciprocity was shown in the 'dance between us composed of minute steps and movements'; in the therapist's actively participating in rolling the car back to Sula; in the therapist's amplifying and extending Sula's noises; in the to and fro of a battle for control. The establishment of an internal containing object came later in the therapy, in the second phase. Containment and reciprocity are not mutually exclusive. For Sula, the establishment of a responsive object was probably the precursor for improvement.

David Trevatt (1999) described how he had to modify his psycho-analytic technique with Michael, aged five years, who had been inconsistently cared for by his mother, taken into foster care, and then physically and sexually abused by his foster carers. The therapist surprised himself by noticing that he had become much more respon-sive in order to reach Michael.

He found that his usual type of interpretations made no impact on Michael. 'Michael was in need of someone who could help him play and discover what could be achieved through play that had been absent in the vital early years. The form of play which Michael developed was one that required a mindful presence who was often employed by Michael to play by proxy for him' (Trevatt, 1999, p. 286). Trevatt gives several instances of playing by proxy, pointing out the presence of projective identification and projection. He was active in containing powerful projections from Michael. In the following segment, the therapist shows how active he has become and how he and his young patient are working together. 'I fought on by his side.'

I said he looked rather fed up. Michael approached his box and took out his ruler. He hit it against the bank of boxes and then against a badge he was wearing in a tapping motion. He started to look a bit brighter and more focussed and he ordered me to 'Go and stand over there!' He pointed to the corner of the room. Michael said he was bringing me the red felt pen and I was Mrs Parker (the foster-mother who had abused him. This was the first direct reference he had made to these experiences).

Michael showed me where he wanted me to strike at the wall as if hitting Mrs Parker. He told me to 'Start doing it! . . . Go on!' –

and I did so. While making these actions I asked him why I was fighting her and he said she was horrible. I continued fighting and said 'You're horrible Mrs Parker!' I fought on and asked Michael what made her so horrible. He said, 'She smacks children!' He got up on the desk and said he was fighting Mrs Parker's baddies. He hit out with his ruler and occasionally announced that he had killed one. He said that she told lies about children and did not buy them any presents when it is their birthday or at Christmas. I repeated all these statements to my adversary as I fought on by his side.

(Trevatt, 1999, p. 283)

Playing by proxy requires a responsive *and* containing object acting out the dreaded situation without anything terrible happening, so that a detoxified projection can be introjected (taken back in). The therapist needs to show that he can be responsive within the to and fro of the play, the rhythm of the play, and the emotional tone of the play. 'Michael expressed satisfaction at some of the delivery of this creative role as I looked for the right tone of doubt and scorn that he appeared to desire' (Trevatt, 1999, p. 276). Trevatt designates this as projective identification, but in order for this to become manifest within the therapy, the therapist has to be in a reciprocal relationship so that it can be played out. 'He kept a close eye on the direction to make sure I had it exactly right so that I could give form to the unthinkable thought about his suffering at the hands of his abusers' (Trevatt, 1999, p. 277). This requires the process of projective identification and containment as well as reciprocity.

Freud's observation of his grandson playing with the cotton reel (Freud, 1920/1991) was a fundamental contribution to the idea of the importance of play. He observed his grandchild playing a game of disappearance and return, which Freud felt was related to how the boy coped with brief separations of a few hours from his mother.

What he did was to hold the reel by the string and very skilfully throw it over the edge of his curtained cot, so that it disappeared into it, at the same time uttering his expressive 'o-o-o-o'. He then pulled the reel out of the cot again by the string and hailed its reappearance with a joyful 'da' (there).

(Freud, 1920/1991, p. 284)

However, here the child could approach the thought of his separation from his mother in play by himself, presumably because he had robust internal objects. Michael, however, needed someone else to act out the dreaded situation, so that the other could contain the disturbing thoughts and emotions.

Anne Alvarez alluded to reciprocity in her description of work with autistic children:

> In the Tavistock Autism Workshop we have learned nowadays to be more gently active, to try and get eye contact where we can do so tactfully, maybe occasionally to 'chase' the child a little, without being too intrusive . . . most of this sensing of distance, of tone of voice, speed and pitch of speech, comes quite naturally to people when they speak to tiny babies.
>
> (Alvarez, 1999, p. 56)

This type of reciprocity is deliberate and is used with cut-off children. It requires the therapist to be very active in the sequence of reciprocity, especially in the initial stages of initiation, orientation, state of attention and acceleration. With a withdrawn child and a therapist, both 'partners' may not be participating in this social sequence: the whole cycle may be carried out by the therapist alone. The deliberate amplification of the cycle by the therapist is an attempt to engage the withdrawn child in a reciprocal interaction.

In another paper, Alvarez described the process of getting in touch with her patient, Robbie, and there was a moment when there was contact between them, which I think was an amplification of the initial stages of reciprocity.

> I would suggest that the strength of feeling I felt and conveyed on that July day, however melodramatic, unbalanced, uncontained and uncontaining it may seem, did have something to do with a reach which was simply, for once, long enough, or loud enough, or alerting enough or human enough to get his attention.
>
> (Alvarez, 1992, p. 84)

Judith Jackson despaired of being able to reach her patient, a violent boy (Jackson, 1999). Suddenly, the boy began to imitate her, and in response she imitated him, a reciprocal interaction. He was delighted and there was a pause in the session, together with a rare feeling of closeness. Interestingly, imitation is part of Bion's theory of thinking (Bion, 1962a), where, through imitation, the therapist and patient are both disclosing their knowledge and observation of each other, which could be said to be a function of reciprocity.

Bartram (1999), in her description of her psychoanalytic psycho-therapeutic work, used Brazelton's theory of reciprocity to describe her interaction with Sean, aged three years. Sean had developed normally up to the age of 18 months, when he began to withdraw into himself after his family had suffered a traumatic loss. In the sessions, Sean would jump off the table when she counted to three, using the game to adapt to each other. 'Periods of prolonged and intense eye contact developed' (Bartram, 1999, p. 138). 'This game had the natural form of mother–infant interactions as described by Brazelton et al. involving the stages of initiation acceleration, peak of excitement (at the "threeeee") and finally deceleration' (Bartram, 1999, p. 138).

Bartram highlighted the intense and primitive feelings she experienced. 'At the moment of re-finding each other I felt a great and unexpected rush of feeling and easily *betrayed* [my emphasis] my delight in re-encountering him through my words, my voice and doubtless through my facial expression and body language' (Bartram, 1999, p. 139). Note the use of the word 'betrayed'; that is, the therapist feels that she should not be doing this.

This is a rare example of a psychoanalytic psychotherapist being aware of the concept of reciprocity informing her actions. Consciously knowing about the concept enables the possibility of that knowledge informing practice. Reciprocity is fundamental to relationships, social communication and emotional regulation. Therefore one could assume that this knowledge would be a therapeutic asset in work with children experiencing difficulty in those areas. This will be discussed in more detail later.

Susan Reid (1990) described the primitive nature of an interaction and her intuitive response to Georgie, a boy aged two years and one month in foster care. Georgie had had an inappropriately responding mother, in that she was mentally ill. She had times of tormenting him and times of being withdrawn. The following description comes from his second session with his therapist. (The descriptions are taken from her draft paper, where the descriptions are much more immediate.)

> Feeling the measure of his terror my body responds to him before my mind can have thoughts about it. I understand that he cannot tolerate words and I, anyway, cannot find any. I manage to stand almost perfectly still and respond by humming to him. Over minutes his body relaxes its grip and when the time feels right, I add words to the hum. It becomes a lullaby in which I use his name and sing of his fear.
>
> (Reid, 1990, p. 3)

Georgie was then able to loosen his grip on her, get down and approach his box. This is a compressed example of both reciprocity and containment. Reid's description shows how she has an experience of his emotional communication and then moderates the feeling. Clearly, a careful processing of containment is occurring here, continually modulated by awareness and thought. But it begins with something that comes in a rush, prior to thought. The elements of an immediate, primitive and appropriate response by the body before the mind can consciously think and the use of a verbal response without words (humming) established a reciprocal object which then enabled the creation of a containing object. Indeed, containment predicates a relationship, because it requires two people in communication with each other.

Another example from Susan Reid's paper occurred after two months of therapy.

> Georgie . . . went straight to his box and rummaged inside (unusual) . . . he is looking for something and I wait full of curiosity. Georgie takes out his perspex ball which had a colourful butterfly inside . . . he holds it up for me to see and smiling full at me places it with exquisite care onto the floor and gently rolls it sucking in and holding his breath as he does so. I find it impossible to convey in words the beauty of the moment . . . I am reminded of an early childhood experience . . . I am too full to speak, so nod at him to convey my feelings of sharing the experience.
>
> (Reid, 1990, p. 10)

Georgie then moves to play a game with her, losing and finding the ball, reminiscent of the cotton reel game from Freud. He 'repeats the game over and over again'. The therapist gives him a long interpretation, but 'in manageable amounts and I was surprised by his wish to listen and my feeling that we understood one another'. A week later, he began to use words for the first time and soon began to feel like a human baby rather than a little animal. This sequence illustrates a process of reverie as the therapist waits, not just attentively, but also full of curiosity. There is contact between them, a shared experience full of emotion, which develops into a game. This then becomes available for interpretation. I think containment and reciprocity are intertwined here, both having been established in earlier sessions. The ball as a container is in evidence at the beginning of the sequence. Major changes occurred after this session.

Ann Wells (1997) described therapy with Helen, aged six years. Helen was characterised as being severely mentally handicapped. She had been born after a two-day labour with the cord around her neck. She was placed in a special baby unit, although her mother could not remember for how long. She had suffered chronic sexual abuse and also had had numerous admissions to hospital for serious illnesses. The therapist characterised the first months of therapy thus:

> Mothers by their words and actions provide a patterned context for their baby's sounds and movements. These patterns are sometimes active, sometimes soothing; out of them develops mutual communication and, eventually, language. The baby-in-bits in my room had to be shown that an object existed, in relationship and communication with her (Alvarez, 1992). My role with Helen in the first instance was to draw attention to the potential meaningfulness of her experiences and actions. Only after such attention and sorting have been integrated can the other sophisticated aspects of interpretation, such as the location of a feeling or the reason for it, be approached.
>
> (Wells, 1997, p. 105)

I would suggest that the therapist is talking about the necessity of establishing a responsive object in the first instance.

In the ninth session, Wells described the following:

> I found myself automatically behaving like a mother who does not expect her child to understand language. Thus, when she drops the doll and leans down to look for it, I feel impelled to pick it up and in fact, am doing so before I can think and can only retrospectively talk of what has happened . . . my automatic retrieving of the doll delighted Helen.
>
> (Wells, 1997, p. 107)

It can be seen in the examples quoted above that one of the features of these moments of interaction seems to be that therapists express surprise that they have acted in this way. Another feature is that they seem to react unconsciously, or automatically. This will be discussed later.

The following extract is from Waddell (1998), who uses an observation by Shuttleworth:

Mother put her baby to the breast. He sucked steadily making snuffly noises. He seemed quite relaxed, but then suddenly coughed, continued to suck for a moment and then began to cry. Mother sat him up on her lap to wind him. He was giving thin, high cries followed by a few sobs. He moved his head from side to side. His face was pink and puckered. This behaviour would stop and he would relax for a time and then repeat it. He didn't bring up any wind. He didn't ever cry wholeheartedly, just in this spasmodic way. Mother lifted him to her shoulder and his shrieks increased. She put him on his tummy on her knee and he still shrieked, throwing his head back. She sat him up for a while saying that this is how he felt most comfortable. All the while she was talking to him soothingly. She told the observer that one could feel how stiff his legs and tummy were. She decided to put him back to the breast 'to see if that would help'. The baby sucked quite eagerly and seemed to relax. He dozed off. She held him in that position for a little while and then, as she moved him, he woke up. She sat him up to wind him. He brought up some wind. He sat in his mother's lap looking sleepy, his head nodding forward. But when she offered him the breast again to see if he was still hungry, he sucked noisily, his cheeks going in and out at a furious rate. The rest of him was quite still. He gradually slowed down and stopped feeding. Then he lay back in his mother's arms and gazed at her face. She smiled and talked to him. He cooed in reply and waved his hands (Shuttleworth, 1998).

(Waddell, 1998, p. 29)

This example shows how containment by the mother sets the scene for reciprocity at the end of this vignette. During initiation, the baby 'lay back in his mother's arms' in order to be able to move to the next stage of orientation (gazed at her face) and state of attention, moving to acceleration (he cooed in reply) and peak of excitement (waved his hands). Waddell used the example to illustrate containment and thus concentrated on the segment of interaction before the reciprocal interaction at the end. She pointed out how the mother was able to engage with the baby's anxiety, speaking to him soothingly and gently trying different physical positions to find one that he was comfortable in. The mother was able to tolerate his anxiety and to manage it until the baby could manage the distress himself. Once this occurred, he was available for engagement in a reciprocal interaction at the end of the segment. So, for some children, containment precedes a reciprocal interaction. For other children, such as Robbie, whose therapy with

Anne Alvarez (Alvarez, 1992) was described earlier, a very active reciprocal interaction was required in order to bring him into contact with another human being.

Urban (1999) described an assessment for autism in a boy.

> Tim, aged 7, was being asked questions by my psychiatrist colleague about what others might think . . . Tim couldn't do this, and seemed to feel intimidated and angry. He took the toy he was holding and repeatedly thrust it toward her face. *Without thinking* [my emphasis], I matched what I said with the rhythm and aggressive thrust of his actions; 'Tim! doesn't! like-it! when-he! can't! answer! questions!' When I did he looked directly at me with sparkling eyes, turned and did it again to my accompaniment.
>
> (Urban, 1999, p. 8)

Urban used this as an example of amodal perception. This is linked to Stern's attunement, as discussed earlier, where he emphasised the adult demonstrating understanding of the affect underlying the action of the child by communicating through a different modality from the one the child is using. So, in this example, the boy used non-verbal physical actions, whereas the therapist used verbal actions (rhythm, intonation and words) to represent the communication. This type of amodal representation is often seen in Beatrice Beebe's work. As well as being an example of reciprocity, this segment also illustrates reciprocity happening unconsciously, 'without thinking', as Elizabeth Urban put it.

Reid (1997) described an infant observation of a boy, Freddie, who developed autistic defences in the face of a mother who was overwhelmed by having three children and was unresponsive to him. Although she mentions Brazelton, Reid used the study to concentrate on Tronick's concept of mutual affect regulation (a reciprocity-related concept). Reid summarised Tronick's work on the importance of responsivity and also on the effects of non-reciprocal interactions, illustrating this point with a moment from the observation when Freddie was seven months old:

> She then turns and puts him on her knee in the usual way. Freddie arches his back and turns his face towards her. He reaches his little hand up to his mother's cheek and tries for some time to turn her face towards him, but mum seems distracted, first

by his brother and sister fighting and squabbling and then by her own thoughts and she begins to chat distractedly.

(Reid, 1997, p. 68)

Reid related the observations of Freddie's responses to his unresponsive mother to those described by Tronick of infants faced with the 'still-face' experiments. In these experiments, the infant's responses are recorded when the mother is instructed to keep her face impassive (e.g., Murray (1991); this is described in more detail later. These infants lost their posture, withdrew and showed self-comforting behaviour, which Freddie also exhibited as his mother continually failed to attend to him. This infant observation took place as part of a psychoanalytic infant observation seminar. In her discussion of the observation, Reid used Tronick's work to explain Freddie's development of autistic-like features as a result of the failure of the mother's capacity to understand Freddie's emotional communications and to respond to them. She did not link his work to the psychoanalytic concept of containment, perhaps because she was trying to introduce his work to a psychoanalytic audience, thereby concentrating on the child development concept, and her secondary focus was on the link to autism. However, this paper represents one of the few attempts within the psychoanalytic literature to use the child development concept of reciprocity or a reciprocity-related concept to explain the findings.

Besnard et al. (1998) observed a boy, Maxime, when he was eight days old, at home with his mother. Maxime had been watching the observer and his mother talk together and had fallen asleep.

A few moments later he wakes up. He tries to open his eyes, then closes them again. He repeats this sequence several times. Then his facial expressions become more noticeable, his face puckers, he begins to utter little cries and to wriggle about. He puckers his face even more, his hands twist, his arms begin to flail about, and he starts to cry. Mme Martine arrives with the feeding bottle. She speaks to him reassuringly and lifts him up. Maxime stops crying at once. He immediately relaxes and looks intently at his mother. Mme Martin is still talking to him, telling him how like his father he is – like him, not very lucky as far as hair is concerned! Maxime is very much in contact with his mother; he looks as though he's devouring her with his eyes.

(Besnard et al., 1998, p. 53)

This segment illustrates both containment and reciprocity, although the containment is more of the Bick type of soothing containment. The mother notices that Maxime is upset after waking up, talks to him and calms him down. This is very effective as he 'immediately relaxes' and then orients to her, the beginnings of the cycle of reciprocity. He looks at her intently, his mother talks to him, and the intensity of their contact appears to deepen: 'he looks as though he's devouring her with his eyes.' It would be interesting to have a microanalysis of a video of them at this point to see the details of their interaction together, but one would predict that their eye contact and non-verbal interaction would be reciprocal.

One of the features of these moments of interaction seems to be that therapists express surprise that they have acted in this way. There are several reasons for this. First, the process has not yet been named properly, so that even though it must often occur, there is not yet the language within psychoanalysis to think about it. The second reason is that a lot of therapists think that they should not be doing it, and their first reaction is to eschew it. This was also the case with the concepts of transference and then counter-transference (Heimann, 1950), where the phenomenon is first thought of as a hindrance, but is then thought about further and is described, named and placed within a theoretical framework, creating the concept. The third reason is that suddenly to have a primitive feeling of closeness is surprising.

There may be different aspects of reciprocity that need further elaboration and clarification, such as the very deliberate nature of building reciprocal interactions with autistic children. Another aspect seems to be that some interactions characterised by reciprocity are intuitive. They are immediate, intense and at a deep level of feeling and contact.

It has been possible to identify reciprocity within the work of psychoanalytic psychotherapists. There appear to be some specific features of the experience of reciprocity within the therapy room. Therapists express surprise to find that they have interacted with a child in this way. They seem to be acting unconsciously or automatically within the relationship with the child. They recognise a qualitative difference in this type of interaction compared to how they 'normally' act within the therapeutic situation. They generally do not have a name for this experience. They notice a feeling of closeness with the child. There appear to be different aspects of reciprocity, as though reciprocity is on a continuum, from the deliberate nature of building a reciprocal interaction with an autistic child to an intuitive, intense interaction.

6   Does containment occur in child development research?

Finding detailed observations of mother–infant interactions in the literature of child development research was surprisingly difficult, even though research on the capacity of infants to interact continues to increase. The original paper by Brazelton incorporates examples, as do other older papers, when microanalysis of filmed interactions began. However, most recent papers now refer to microanalysis as an accepted research method and do not include any of the original observations. For instance, an examination of the past three years (2000–3) of the *Infant Mental Health Journal* yields only Beebe's work as including examples and an examination of two years (2001–2) of *Infancy, the Journal of the International Society of Infant Studies* yielded no examples, even though many researchers are using microanalysis in their research. They tend to refer only briefly to the methodology, perhaps because it is so prevalent now, and to present aggregated results rather than a detailed description of an interaction, which is required in order for the data to be interrogated. Examples have therefore had to be found in older work, in contrast to the previous section on examining examples from psychoanalytic publications that have been published within the past five years. Even older literature presents aggregated data. For example, in the 1987 version of the *Handbook of Infant Development* (Osofsky, 1987), none of the chapters that include analysis of parent–infant interactions gives any examples in prose, apart from one very brief example from Papousek, which is referred to later.

Some of the examples in Osofsky (1987) are descriptive, but in a presentation that, again, makes it difficult to interrogate the data. For example, Sackett (1987) described an interaction as follows!

The most probable maternal behaviours occurring simultaneously (lag 0) with infant NONE are LOOK and TOUCH-PLAY, with mother VOC markedly inhibited. No signal (NONE) by the mother is inhibited over the total lag range. At lag 1, only mother VOC occurs at an excited level. At lag 3, both mother VOC and TOUCH-PLAY are excited.

(Sackett, 1987, p. 870)

The only chapter that does contain descriptive material is one on clinical examples by Cramer (1987) which is not relevant to this particular chapter looking at child development research.

Another difficulty is that containment is difficult to observe. Currently, there are no studies that used video to describe the observable aspects of containment. Trowell (2003) suggested that it may be possible to study the eyes of the participants by microanalysis. I propose to look for the presence of containment by identifying various behaviours in the descriptions. The baby quietens in the presence of an adult who is showing calm attention. The baby is able to change its behaviour after the strength of its emotion has decreased with an adult who is calmly attending to the baby. The adult shows that they can tolerate the emotions of the baby, neither ignoring it nor retaliating. In terms of containment, the adult is showing that they can experience to some degree the emotional communication of the infant, that they are not overwhelmed by it, are able to process the experience and communicate this back to the baby.

It is difficult to know whether to put Beebe's work in the previous chapter or in this chapter, as her work is explicitly integrative in nature; that is, it integrates different interventions from different theoretical viewpoints. She uses the microanalysis of videotaped interactions in her therapeutic work with families, integrating it with interpretation and understanding the transference. She does briefly include a consideration of containment in her work; for example, 'my role was to "hold" or "contain" this aggression without interpreting it or retaliating' (Beebe, 2003, p. 44). However, I am going to include her in this child development chapter because the idea of containment is not central to her work (she is an American working in New York, where, as discussed previously, containment is not routinely used as a concept), and her way of working is more nested within research method, although the use of video feedback in interventions does seem to be spreading out from the research community.

This observation is taken from Beebe's work when Johann was seven months old.

Johann was looking down, fingering the cloth of the infant seat. I was quiet. He looked briefly, and I said 'Hi (pause), hi (pause)' with a soft, sinusoidal contour. He looked down, then looked at me for five seconds, with a small partial smile, as I moved my head up and down slightly, saying 'Hi, hi.' He looked down and fingered the cloth. His hand then gently and repeatedly hit the arm of the infant seat. Meanwhile I was silent, not moving. Johann looked at me for four seconds, looked at the ceiling, then looked at me again with a small kicking movement. I briefly matched the kicking movement with a similar rhythm in my own body, but did not vocalize, Johann looked for six seconds, while I did this and smiled briefly. Then he looked down, fingered the cloth, then gently hit the side of the chair with his hand, while I became quiet. He fingered the cloth, then looked up at me. I vocalized in a rhythm that matched that of his hand hitting the side of the chair. Johann sustained this gaze at me for 26 seconds, while we engaged in an alternating dialogue, each matching the other's rhythm, Johann by gently hitting the chair, and I by vocalizing.

(Beebe, 2003, p. 39)

In the 'Hi, hi' sequence, there are elements of reciprocity in the orientation of the actors to each other and in the rhythm matching. It is also present in the look-away part of the cycle, when Johann looked down, but allowing this recuperation in the look-away part of the dance of reciprocity then promoted a longer sustained contact of 26 seconds. Stern's cross-modal attunement can be seen. This is a feature of Beebe's work. It can be seen here when, for instance, Johann hit the side of the chair with his hand and Beebe matches the rhythm with her voice. Elements of containment would be easier to identify with descriptions of the affect of the participants, but perhaps the presence of containment can be inferred from the behaviour of the therapist where she writes at three points that she became quiet; 'meanwhile I was silent, not moving . . . but did not vocalize . . . while I became quiet.' It may be that at these points she was containing some emotion or anxiety for Johann, in the sense that Bick uses the concept of containment, to soothe or calm, although, without the description of affect of the two participants, it is difficult to examine.

Later, when Johann was nine months old, Beebe described another interaction.

Mother hid her own face in 'peek-a-boo' and Johann looked at her, with a partial smile. Mother then made a movement in close toward Johann's face, to hide his face in the peek-a-boo game, and he made a sudden, sharp movement of his head down, ducking mother's approach. Mother said 'OK', and pulled back immediately. Johann then frantically arched 90 degrees, and mother stayed quiet and waited. Johann then hung over the edge of the stroller, limp. Then he fussed strongly. Mother said, 'I'm sorry', matching the rhythm of the fuss.

Now Johann looked at mother as she began to play patty-cake. Johann sustained a long gaze, his body moved excitedly, and he joined mother by moving his body in the rhythm of her patty-cake. Then Johann became fussy again, tried to get out of the stroller, and pushed against the strap. Mother vocally matched the infant's distress sounds, and tolerated the distress without moving in, or requesting that he do anything different.

(Beebe, 2003, p. 42)

In this example, the mother was able to recognise Johann's signal of sharply moving his head away. He was overwhelmed and moved to reduce the stimulation. She had been too intrusive in her movement towards Johann's face, but she was able to repair this, pulling back and waiting for him to recover. The segment where he fussed and she said she was sorry to him, matching the rhythm of his fuss, links to reciprocity and Stern's cross-modal attunement. It would be interesting to know more about the quality of the mother's voice in talking to Johann about being sorry, because this is probably an example of her containing his anxiety, restoring his ability to think and to interact, so that they could play patty-cake together. Another aspect of containment, in the sense of being open to projections, or in a state of reverie, may be indicated by the description, 'mother stayed quiet and waited'. Containment may also link to the final sequence where Johann tried to get out of his pushchair and was distressed, but his mother tolerated his anxiety and communicated her understanding by matching his distress sounds. This also links to attunement and mutual affect regulation. This segment highlights the link between the concept of containment and the reciprocity-related concepts of attunement and mutual affect regulation.

Brazelton et al. (1974) filmed the interaction between the mother and child, but also the reaction of the child as a toy monkey on a string moved towards him, dangled within his reach space, and then moved away again. This happened once a week between the ages of four and 20 weeks.

The infant stared fixedly at the object with wide eyes, fixating on it for as much as 2 minutes, by 6 weeks, without disruption of gaze or of attention. In this period, his face was fixed, the muscles of his face tense in a serious set, with eyes staring and mouth and lips protruding toward the object. This static, fixed look of attention was interspersed with little jerks of facial muscles. His tongue jerked out toward the object and then withdrew rapidly. Occasional short bursts of vocalizing toward the object occurred. During these long periods of attention, the eyes blinked occasionally in single, isolated blinks. The body was set in a tense, immobilized sitting position, with the object at his midline. When the object was moved to one side or the other, the infant tended to shift his body appropriately, so it was kept at his midline. His shoulders hunched as if he were about to 'pounce.' . . . Extremities were fixed, flexed at elbow and knee, and fingers and toes were aimed toward the object. Hands were semiflexed or tightly flexed, but fingers and toes repeatedly jerked out to point at the object. Jerky swipes of an arm or leg in the direction of the object occurred from time to time as the period of intense attention was maintained. . . . In this period, his attention seemed 'hooked' on the object, and all his motor behaviour alternated between the long, fixed periods of tense absorption and short bursts of jerky, excited movement which might break into this prolonged state of attention.

(Brazelton et al., 1974, p. 53)

This frame-by-frame analysis of the infant's relationship with his environment shows how he is very active in taking in information about the object and also in reacting to it. The next section of the description shows how he then adapts his behaviour, for both taking in sensory input and external activity, as he reacts to the nearness of the object.

As the object was gradually brought into reach space, his entire state of communication and behavior changed. His eyes softened and lidded briefly but continued to scan it with the same prolonged attention. His mouth opened as if in anticipation of mouthing it. The tongue came out toward it and occasionally remained out for a period before it was withdrawn. His neck arched forward as his head strained towards the object. His shoulders were hunched, and his mouth protruded. Swipes of the arms and extensions of the legs at the knee increased in number. Hands alternately fisted and opened in jerky movements toward the object, there was a very rapid flexor jerk of the extremity, as if extension were first preceded by an involuntary flexor jerk. . . . As he mastered extensor activity, by 16 weeks, this early signature of intention became lost. In an attempt to anchor one hand in order to reinforce the efforts of the other, he often grasped his chair, held onto a piece of his clothing or a part of himself, or put his thumb in his mouth. This seemed to free the other hand to reach unilaterally, at a time when bilateral arm and hand activity is still predominant (10 to 20 weeks), and was comparable to a kind of 'place holding.' Long before reaches could be completed successfully, these segments of such an intention were part of the prolonged states of attention toward the object.

(Brazelton et al., 1974, p. 54)

The next section shows how the infant reaches a peak of excitement, which he then downregulates from in several ways.

This state of intense, rapt attention built up gradually to a peak which was disrupted suddenly by the infant's turning away from the object, becoming active, and flailing his extremities. He often cried out, breathed rapidly, and looked around the room as if to find relief by looking at something else. When he found another object, such as a door or a corner of the room, he latched onto it. He often looked down or closed his eyes in this interval, as if he were processing information about the object in this period of withdrawal. This flailing activity of body, arms and legs was accompanied by facial activity, and he seemed to be 'letting off steam.' The period of disruption was followed by a turning back to the object and a resumption of the 'hooked' state of attention.

(Brazelton et al., 1974, p. 54)

This interaction with an external object has some elements from the pattern of reciprocity observed in the interaction between the infant and his mother, a state of attention building up to a peak, followed by the look-away cycle as the infant downregulates and processes the interaction. However, it does not have the same quality of the dance of reciprocity, as two sentient beings continually adjust to each other. It is interesting to note that in the dance of reciprocity the next step after the peak of excitement is deceleration before the look-away phase. However, with the toy, the next step after the peak of excitement is suddenly turning away. This is probably because in the dance of reciprocity the adult is helping the infant to downregulate so that the infant can move more gradually into the turning-away phase. Beebe and Lachmann (2002) showed that both the mother and the infant respond to each other, literally, within a split second. Both partners adjust to each other within a time range that varies from almost simultaneous through microseconds up to half a second. In relation to the toy, the infant has to regulate himself, so that he suddenly jerks away from the object in order to bring himself down from a high arousal level. This is in contrast to the next passage, in which the mother is helping her baby regulate his arousal level.

In the section of Brazelton et al.'s paper describing the infant's interaction with his mother, rather than with a toy, we read as follows:

> A mother's eyes and lips widen and close in rhythmic movements designed alternately to alert and soothe her baby. As he quiets, her vocalizations and facial movements become rhythmic and 'holding,' and then speed up with more staccato and a faster pace. Her eyes alternately narrow and widen, bright and dull in a measure appropriate to his state. When he overreacts, her eyes take on a soothing look, becoming wider and brighter, to attract and 'hold' his attention.
>
> (Brazelton et al., 1974, p. 66)

In this segment, Brazelton could be describing some non-verbal aspects of containment, especially where he used 'holding' as a description. The microanalysis shows the importance of the mother's eyes to soothe the baby. Brazelton showed how the mother used her eyes to regulate the interaction with the baby, becoming bright or dull according to the needs of the baby. The mother's internal emotional state is not described, but one might conjecture that the rapid changes in the appearance of her eyes reflect the fluctuations in her own emotional state as she perceives the baby's emotional state, processes it, and responds to him appropriately. The concept of containment, as pointed out in the introduction, is usually described as downregulating an emotion, but here the mother is both downregulating and upregulating, as in mutual affect regulation.

In the above interaction, the mother soothed the baby. But in the previous interaction between the baby and the toy monkey, an adult was not available to help the infant control his arousal level. The infant found a way of soothing himself. There appears to be a relationship between self-soothing and containment. As the intense attention of the infant to the monkey built to a peak, it seemed to become too much for him to manage and he started to become distressed. Then, in order to calm down, his eyes sought an object, such as a door.

> He often cried out, breathed rapidly, and looked around the room as if to find relief by looking at something else. When he found another object, such as a door or a corner of the room, he latched onto it. He often looked down or closed his eyes in this interval, as if he were processing information about the object in this period of withdrawal.
>
> (Brazelton et al., 1974, p. 54)

After a period of withdrawal, he was then able to turn back to the toy monkey. It was as if he were containing his own emotions and was then able to 'think' again or interact with the object. The theory of containment would predict that an experience of containment is required in order to be able to contain oneself, creating an internal relationship with an internalised container.

The following example from Stern has already been used to illustrate aspects of reciprocity, but it is repeated here in order to discern whether any elements of containment are present in this description by a child development researcher.

> Joey is sitting on his mother's lap facing her. She looks at him intently but with no expression on her face, as if she were preoccupied and absorbed in thought elsewhere. At first, he glances at the different parts of her face but finally looks into her eyes.
>
> He and she remain locked in a silent mutual gaze for a long moment. She finally breaks it by easing into a slight smile. Joey quickly leans forward and returns her smile. They smile together; or rather, they trade smiles back and forth several times.
>
> Then Joey's mother moves into a gamelike sequence. She opens her face into an expression of exaggerated surprise, leans all the way forward and touches her nose to his, smiling and making bubbling sounds all the while. Joey explodes with delight but closes his eyes when their noses touch. She then reels back, pauses to increase the suspense and sweeps forward again to touch noses. Her face and voice are even more full of delight and 'pretend' menace. This time Joey is both more tense and excited. His smile freezes. His expression moves back and forth between pleasure and fear.

Joey's mother seems not to have noticed the change in him. After another suspenseful pause she makes a third nose-to-nose approach at an even higher level of hilarity and lets out a rousing 'oooOH!' Joey's face tightens. He closes his eyes and turns his head to one side. His mother realises that she has gone too far and stops her end of the interaction too. At least for a moment she does nothing. Then she whispers to him and breaks into a warm smile. He becomes re-engaged.

(Stern, 1998, p. 56)

The second sentence of this sequence may describe the containment-related state of maternal reverie, as the mother looks at her son intently, but quietly, waiting. However, it is not clear, because it is as if 'she were preoccupied and absorbed in thought elsewhere', and to be consonant with the concept of maternal reverie, she would need to be mindfully present in the situation. As Joey signals his readiness to engage by looking into her eyes, she reacts to him. As the interaction progresses, his mother increases her intensity, but this increases Joey's anxiety, which she does not notice. When she does notice, she does nothing for a moment, then 'whispers' and 'breaks into a warm smile'. I propose that it is during the time that she is whispering and smiling that she is containing his anxiety, enabling him to re-engage with her, in Bion's sense, restoring his ability to think, so that instead of being immobilised by his reaction to his anxiety, he can come out and play again, as shown by 'He becomes re-engaged'.

Tronick used Brazelton's concept of reciprocity to develop his idea of mutual affect regulation. In this sequence, he described the interaction between an infant, his caretaker and an object.

The six-month-old infant stretches his hands out toward the object. Because he cannot get hold of it, he becomes angry and distressed. He looks away for a moment and sucks on his thumb. Calmer, he looks back at the object and reaches for it once more. But this attempt fails too, and he gets angry again. The caretaker watches for a moment, then soothingly talks to him. The infant calms down and with a facial expression of interest gazes at the object and makes another attempt to reach for it. . . . The caretaker is responsible for the reparation of the infant's failure into success and the simultaneous transformation of his negative emotion into a positive emotion.

(Tronick, 1989, p. 113)

Tronick uses this example to illustrate mutual affect regulation, but this is also an example of containment, where the infant is angry and frustrated, and communicates this to the caretaker, who understands and communicates back the emotion-become-manageable 'soothingly', and the infant calms down and then is able to try again to reach out. There therefore appears to be a link between affect regulation and containment, and this will be explored in more detail later. One difference between containment and affect regulation is that Tronick does not use the underpinning ideas from psychoanalytic theory that try to explain the mechanisms underlying containment, namely, projection, introjection and projective identification. Thus, Tronick writes that the caretaker transforms the emotions, but the process of transformation is unknown and not described. The other difference is that affect regulation is concerned with the transformation of negative affect into positive affect, whereas containment is more about processing the emotion, no matter what it is, into a manageable form of itself, not necessarily turning it into a 'positive' affect. Thus, one can be angry or sad or guilty, but with the thought that these emotions can be experienced without being overwhelming. It may be that as a result of this the emotion becomes 'positive', that is, in the example above, the anger and distress of the infant subsided, creating both psychic and neurobiological room for another emotion, that of curiosity so that the infant could explore again, but containment focuses on the first part of the sequence, so that the anger and distress become manageable, not that they then turn into another emotion. This is reflected in Bion's idea that the mother replaces a fear of death with anxiety-made-manageable.

> From the infant's point of view she should have taken into her, and thus experienced, the fear that the child was dying . . . an understanding mother is able to experience the feeling of dread, that this baby was striving to deal with by projective identification, and yet retain a balanced outlook.
>
> (Bion, 1959, p. 104)

This may then make it possible for other emotions to be experienced, which may be 'positive'.

The other difference is that, from the beginning of life, Tronick proposes that the affect regulation is mutual, that the baby can also work with the mother as well as the mother working with the baby. Containment, however, proposes that it is a one-way street; that the mother contains the baby's emotions, assuming that the baby's mental apparatus is not advanced enough to do this and also that it is unhealthy for the baby even if it were to be able to do this.

Murray (1991) described her earlier work (Murray & Trevarthen, 1985) in looking at how one to two-month-old infants reacted when the experimenters interfered with infant–mother communication. In the 'Interruption', the experimenter would interrupt the interaction between the baby and mother and talk to the mother. In the 'Blank Face', the mother would be instructed to still all her features and adopt a blank face. In the 'Out of Phase Condition', the mother and infant would each react with the other via a picture on a closed-circuit television, but then the television picture of the mother would be delayed slightly, so that the mother the infant saw was out of phase with the real infant.

> During the Interruption, the infant quietened, reduced active communicative gestures and smiling, but watched both mother and experimenter attentively, without distress. In the Blank Face condition, by contrast, the infant first appeared to try to engage more effectively with the other, frowning at her and thrashing his arms in an agitated fashion. When this failed to elicit a response, the infant seemed to reduce his distress by withdrawing from engagement with the outer environment, becoming self-absorbed, and gazing at his hands or looking blankly into space while perhaps fingering his clothes or touching his face. When the mother's communication was caused to be out of phase with the infant behaviour, reactions resembling puzzlement and confusion occurred, which were again followed by avoidance of the mother and self-directed behaviours. Detailed analysis from film showed that in each sequence the infant's behaviour was coherent and highly organised. Changes in the direction of gaze were systematically linked with changes in facial expression and communication, and the patterning of gaze itself was sensitive to the quality of maternal response.
>
> (Murray, 1991, p. 224)

Murray pointed out that the mothers became agitated when the infants became distressed, and when the situation returned to normal, the mothers would try to compensate by being extra-attentive to their children.

One interesting feature of these interactions is that the babies' responses are highly organised in the face of several different disrupted interactions with their mothers. The link to containment may occur after the experimental condition, where the mothers were supposed to follow a protocol and their infants had to manage for themselves, in that afterwards they paid extra attention to their babies. It would be interesting to have more detail about this, as I would hypothesise that this is where the mothers were containing their infants' anxieties about the peculiar nature of the disrupted inter-actions and were moving back to their normal relationship. This might also be a macro-example of rupture and repair, in that rupture and repair usually takes place within seconds or even tenths of a second, but in this experimental condition the rupture and the repair took place over minutes rather than seconds. In the experimental condition where the mother paid attention to someone else, a very usual occurrence in daily life, most of these babies had already devel-oped a way of coping with their mother's attention being directed elsewhere that included remaining attentive, presumably to be ready to resume interaction. The other conditions were not normal with 'normal' mothers, and the babies had to try to cope with the lack of reciprocity.

In her 1991 paper, Murray carried out research with depressed women and non-depressed women and their infants from when the infants were two months old up to 18 months old. She found that the infants of the depressed mothers were more hesitant and depressed and showed more displacement activities than the babies of non-depressed mothers. Murray felt that her findings were in line with object relations theory, in that the depression impaired the ability of the mother to be in a sensitive interaction with her baby, and this, in turn, affected the development of her child. The depression also interfered with the mother's ability to be in a reciprocal interaction with her child, in that the single most predictive factor for the impact of depression upon the child was neither the length nor the severity of the depression, but the degree to which the mother was preoccupied with her own experience rather than the infant's experience. There-fore, the concepts of containment and reciprocity would predict that the child is affected because the mother's preoccupation interferes with her ability to provide both containment for the infant's emotions and reciprocal interactions with her child. This finding is extremely important for those who work with depressed mothers and their children, as it provides a method for selecting those dyads most at risk. It points both to the explanation of why postnatal depression in the mother affects the child and to where we need to aim the inter-vention. This is much more helpful than the blunt instrument of knowing how depressed a mother is or for how long she has been depressed. The link with object relations theory in general was that the child's preconception of a containing mother had failed to some extent to be met in the depressed mothers. The link with containment in particular was that the depression impaired the mother's ability to contain her baby's affective states, and this, in turn, meant that the baby's capacity to process his own emotions was impaired.

Murray and Andrews (2000) have taken sequential photographs of babies interacting with the world from birth. One sequence shows baby Ethan. In the first minute and a half from his birth, the captions capture some of the action in the photographs.

> The midwife lifts Ethan and takes him away to check his breathing. Ethan's arm jerks up as he is moved, and he loses his thumb, which he was sucking. He flails around as the wraps are removed. Ethan cries as he is left uncovered in the cot, eyes tightly shut in the glare of the bright light. Having checked Ethan is breathing normally, the midwife can now take Ethan back. Ethan is still distressed as he is passed back to his mother. As he is placed on his mother, the thrashing of his arms is contained. Ethan is wrapped, his arms are tucked in and his distress subsides. Ethan's mother strokes his head and greets him, and he becomes calm. Just a minute since his birth, and Ethan is finally settled, looking comfortable and relaxed as he is held in his mother's arms.
>
> (Murray & Andrews, 2000, p. 22)

In the next 18 seconds, 'Ethan opens his eyes and looks directly at his mother, Julie. He watches her intently, his eyes scanning the details of her face' (Murray & Andrews, 2000, p. 24). There are a few disruptions and the next sequence occurs when he is six and a half minutes old.

> Soon Ethan and his mother are back in contact. The midwife has put Ethan to the breast, but in fact he is not interested in feeding; he wants only to look at Julie's face. Ethan watches his mother intently again. As Julie talks to him, Ethan's face becomes more mobile and expressive. Occasionally Ethan looks around, as there are voices and movements nearby. But he quickly resumes contact with his mother and appears to take real pleasure in engaging with her even making gentle cooing sounds. A little later Ethan notices his father's voice, as John talks to Julie. Ethan turns to look at his father, his face stilling as he listens, then he shifts his gaze back to Julie's face as she replies.
>
> (Murray & Andrews, 2000, p. 26)

In this case, containment of Ethan's distress by his mother preceded their reciprocal interaction, when he is distressed after being moved and put alone, naked, in a strange cot with an unfamiliar bright light overwhelming his visual system. Then his mother strokes him and talks to him, 'he becomes calm', and he enters into an engagement with her. The striking aspect of this description of Ethan is that it powerfully illustrates that he wants to be in contact with his mother, even to the extent of ignoring being fed, and that this occurs within minutes of his being born.

It has been much more difficult to find descriptions of adult–child interactions in the child development literature than in the psychoanalytic psychotherapy literature. However, it has been possible to find examples of containment occurring alongside descriptions of reciprocal interactions. There are several features of containment in these accounts. Firstly, containment occurs within the reciprocal relationship. Secondly, there is a similarity between containment and mutual affect regulation, but there are also differences. The concept of containment is almost always used in situations of downregulation, whereas there is also a need for upregulation. Thirdly, sometimes containment seems necessary in order for the infant to be ready for reciprocity, although at other times this is reversed and reciprocity seems to be necessary for the process of containment to occur. Fourthly, these examples, taken together with the examples used to generate a definition of containment, seem to suggest that there may be a continuum for containment with a link to reciprocity through mutual affect regulation.

7 Are containment and reciprocity linked?

The continuum of containment

It seemed to me, as I examined Bion's writings and contemporary writers on containment, that a continuum of containment emerged. I would therefore like to propose that there are degrees of containment. At one end of the spectrum, it is *as if* there is containment of parts of the self or personality of the other. This occurs in psychotic functioning, or when the mind is very disturbed, and one recourse seems to be to get rid of the offending part of the self: 'This originated in what he felt was my [Bion's] refusal to accept parts of his personality. Consequently, he strove to force them into me with increased desperation and violence' (Bion, 1959, p. 104). In the middle of the spectrum is the containment of intense emotions, which the analyst does for the analysand and the mother does for the infant, while at the other end is the to and fro of less intense emotions, which is strongly related to mutual affect regulation and thereby links to reciprocity. Bion (1970), as quoted earlier, referred to 'the fluctuations which make the analyst at one moment the "container" and the analysand the "contained", and at the next reverse the roles' (Bion, 1970, p. 108), and this can be seen as linking to reciprocity. It is interesting to note that the difference between these two dates indicates again a move from early Bion to late Bion.

These points require naming. In order to facilitate discussion, I propose the terms 'macrocontainment', 'containment' and 'microcontainment' respectively. My assumption is that containment describes an 'as if' situation. That is, an emotion does not fly through the ether from one person to another. Similarly with parts of the personality. Senses and mirror neurons (Kohler et al., 2002) may pick up another's emotional activity and to some degree replicate it, so that one has a sense of it, but this is not the same as a parcel travelling from one to another, so that the other has it now.

Macrocontainment is how containment was described by 'early' Bion (1959) and is used by those working with patients or others who are in the grip of psychotic functioning. This includes the idea of projecting out parts of the personality. This is based on Klein's idea of projective identification (Klein, 1946), where parts of the self are split off and projected. For example, a patient might feel that she is stupid and everyone else is clever, because she has projected out that aspect of herself. Again, I would like to clarify that I mean that it is 'as if' she has projected out part of herself. 'Her therapist may need to explore in herself, then, how it is that this patient always makes her feel so protective and intelligent and wise' (Alvarez, 1992, p. 3).

Containment is how the process is generally conceptualised by psychotherapists in psychoanalytic psychotherapy writings in books and journals, the containment of intense emotions, which the analyst does for the analysand and the mother does for the infant. It is reflected in the definition of containment developed earlier, that containment is thought to occur when one person receives and understands the emotional communication of another without being overwhelmed by it and communicates this back to the other person. This process can restore the capacity to think in the other person. Containment in the middle part of the continuum is about communicating and managing intense anxiety and emotions.

Microcontainment, however, extends the current ideas about containment. It describes the *sharing* of less intense feelings in the second-to-second interplay between two people, where the baby is active in the process as well as the mother, and there is a *mutual* regulation. Microcontainment explicitly includes both positive and negative emotions. It also includes the use of the theoretical mechanisms of projection and introjection by both baby and mother. The concept of projection tends to be used in terms of the totality of one emotion being projected outwards. Within microcontainment, however, it is as if only part of the emotion would be projected outwards, as the emphasis is more on the sharing of an emotion. From evidence described earlier, the conclusion proposed here is that the baby has an innate capacity from birth to relate in this way, or even before, given that the foetus already smiles and cries in the womb from 26 weeks after conception (Campbell, 2004). It may be that the physical containment of the womb and the foetus's own innate capacities enable him to begin to learn about his own emotions and the transition from one state to another in the womb. This would be part of the preconception for a containing object for when he is born and hopefully meets the concept personified so that he can build up a realisation.

Thus, microcontainment is where the baby's rudimentary abilities to contain emotions would enable him to participate in a shared regulation of affect with the mother, presumably as long as the emotions are not too intense to overwhelm his initial ability. This would be similar to mutual affect regulation. Microanalysis of mother–infant interactions (e.g., Beebe & Lachmann, 2002) and descriptions of sessions by child psychotherapists (e.g., Reid, 1990) already show that adults help infants manage intense emotions. Tronick's work shows that infants regulate adults as well as the other way round (e.g., Tronick et al., 1986). But, presumably, infants vary individually in their ability to participate in the containment process, just as athletes vary individually in their zone of optimal functioning with relationship to anxiety (Gould & Tuffey, 1996). More work is needed to describe microcontainment in the infant–adult relationship. One mechanism for this would be through infant observation. Another would be through microanalysis of video material.

Mutual affect regulation and microcontainment have similarities and differences. The differences are that mutual affect regulation describes negative affect being transformed into positive affect through mutual interaction, rather than using the idea from containment that 'negative' affect can be experienced and managed in its own right. Mutual affect regulation does not use Bion's idea of a container or the hypothesised psychoanalytic mechanisms of projection and introjection to describe the process (while the neurobiological evidence for communicative mechanisms builds up).

The continuum of reciprocity

Just as with containment, I found that, as I read the child development research literature, it emerged that reciprocity could also be seen as occurring along a continuum. At one end is the amplified reciprocity described by Alvarez (1992), used to 'reach' children who are impaired in their ability to relate to others, such as children on the autism spectrum. This is usually conscious and deliberate on behalf of one half of the dyad. As discussed previously, for withdrawn children the mother or therapist exaggerates the initial stages of reciprocity (initiation, orientation, state of attention, acceleration) in order to claim the attention of the child. The mismatch between the responsive abilities of the participants may mean that often the therapist or mother dances alone, progressing through the stages in the dance of reciprocity on her own as she attempts to engage the child in a reciprocal interaction.

In the centre is reciprocity as described in the earlier definition. It is characterised by being unconscious and can include feeling intense emotions and a feeling of closeness. This would suggest that this process is involved in bonding and in determining the quality of an attachment. Both partners in the dyad are active participants. It is characterised by elements of musicality: rhythm and a pattern to the dance. It includes the emotions of joy, love and pleasure. It is about relating to each other, finding out about each other (the epistemological instinct). The dance includes the elements of 'rupture and repair' and 'chase and dodge'.

At the other end is the mutual affect regulation aspect of reciprocity, which links to microcontainment. The emphasis is not so much on relating to each other and the pleasure from doing so, as in reciprocity, but on both partners of the dyad being involved with the regulation of emotion between them.

Attunement and intersubjectivity, although both derived from reciprocity, would perhaps lie close to the reciprocity continuum, rather than actually appearing on it. Attunement would cluster around the mutual affect regulation/microcontainment end of the continuum. Even though it is a reciprocity-related concept, it has more in common with containment, in the sense of emphasising that the mother is the active partner not the infant. The mother attunes to the baby rather than the baby attuning to the mother or both partners being actively involved in the process. However, in another way, it is not as close to containment, because containment is to some degree about the regulation of emotion, and processing and managing emotional states, whereas attunement is more about recognising and incorporating different emotional states into one's emotional repertoire. Therefore, attunement is not the same as microcontainment, but it is closely linked.

Intersubjectivity, it seems to me, is a more diffuse concept than reciprocity, as it seems to include many behaviours and intents that are about sharing an experience: to coordinate with feeding and cleaning and to get mother's attention by expressing alarm, hunger or pain; to seek proximity and to watch both verbal and non-verbal signals and become engaged in the process; to respond with pleasure and to use pre-speech movements of lips, tongue and hands and preverbal vocalisations; to exhibit emotions, intent and pleasure in mastery; to engage in reciprocal interaction, which includes the emotional state of the other and where each adjusts to the other; to express distress in the face of threat by the other and confusion if the other's actions cannot be understood; and 'to avoid excessive, insensitive, or unwanted attempts by others to communicate, thus to retain a measure of personal control over one's state of expression to others' (Trevarthen, 1980, p. 327). So, again, even though intersubjectivity is a reciprocity-related concept, it would cluster near the reciprocity continuum, rather than being on it.

The relationship between the two continuums

I propose that the containment and reciprocity continuums are themselves linked to each other. One end of the containment continuum, microcontainment, is closely related to mutual affect regulation. However, it is important not to visualise the two continuums as comprising one straight line with macrocontainment at one end running along into amplified reciprocity at the other, because each continuum is not just a version of the other. The two continuums intersect along a plane, at an angle, where the intersect is at microcontainment and near mutual affect regulation. The continuums can be visualised as a V (see Figure 7.1). Technically, because microcontainment is not the same as mutual affect regulation, the intersect is near mutual affect regulation. These two terms are not synonymous; there are subtle differences between them. This may seem pedantic, but in order to create an

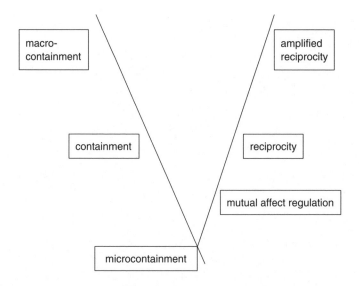

Figure 7.1 To show the relationship between the containment and reciprocity continuums.

actual intersect between the continuums, I propose that microcontainment is the theoretical construct that lies on both continuums. As a construct, it contains elements of both reciprocity/mutual affect regulation and containment.

The extensions of the two continuums would contain other concepts that I am unaware of, so that the currently visible parts of the continuums would be the sections defined in this book.

I think that the containment continuum is defined by the degree of projection from parts of the personality to intense, often difficult emotions to the to and fro of sharing more manageable emotions, which are sometimes positive ones. It can also be defined by the intensity of affect from containment to microcontainment. The reciprocity continuum is defined in another plane. This plane is perhaps characterised by the degree to which the process occurs within the unconscious mind. Amplified reciprocity would tend to be used by the conscious mind, and reciprocity is used by both, while mutual affect regulation tends to be used more by the unconscious. Both planes intersect at microcontainment, where the intensity of affect is low, and it tends to be used more by the unconscious mind.

The two concepts of reciprocity and containment are thus both different and related, as they intersect at microcontainment.

8   What are their differences and similarities?

In his 2001 paper, Trevarthen examined child development research, attachment research and psychodynamic theories. Apart from summarising the research showing that babies are born ready to relate, he also captured the essence of the difference between psychodynamic containment theories and reciprocity theories.

> None of these portraits (psychodynamic theories) takes full account of the young infant's sensitive and joyful appreciation of expression in the human voice, nor were infants' sensitive and gestural behaviours noticed that are adapted to 'talk to' the ongoing imaginations and narratives of purpose that are implicit in talk and gesture addressed to them by their playful parents.
>
> (Trevarthen, 2001, p. 97)

He also acknowledged that psychodynamic theories were shifting with the increased knowledge available from child development research and that this can be seen in the work of Alvarez (1992) and Stern (1985).

There are similarities and differences between the concepts. Trevarthen emphasises the contribution made by the concept of reciprocity, but, equally, there is also a contribution made by the concept of containment to the description of human interaction, the processing of emotion and regulation of affect, and the description of human development.

Are they the same?

Perhaps the first question to address is the most obvious one of whether these two concepts do in fact describe two different phenomena. Firstly, the concept of containment and the concept of reciprocity differ in the roles they allocate to the mother and the baby. The concept of containment implies fundamentally different roles for the mother and baby. Although the baby is active in the sense of projecting, the mother is the container, not the baby. It is the mother who acts as a container for the baby's projections. Psychoanalytic theory suggests that from this the baby gradually builds up an internal containing object.

> Her thinking transforms the infant's feelings into a known and tolerated experience . . . he will introject and identify with a mother who is able to think, and he will introject also his own now modified feelings. Each such projective–introjective cycle between infant and mother is part of a momentous process which gradually transforms the infant's entire mental situation.
>
> (O'Shaughnessy, 1981, p. 179)

The earlier work of Klein provided the foundation for this. She attempted to describe the situation whereby a baby developed the capacity to manage his own emotions. She postulated that as the baby was able to experience more depressive concern, he became more capable of managing his internal states, and would therefore have less need to project them outwards in order to rid himself of them (Klein, 1958/1988). In essence, this means that instead of simply expelling aggressive feelings, the baby was able to feel concern for the consequence of aggression, moving, in psychoanalytic terms, from a paranoid-schizoid state into a depressive state. The point here is that Klein described the idea that a baby could move into a position of being able to manage his own feelings, but it was Bion who provided the theoretical mechanism for the transformation of the emotions and anxiety in the concept of containment; how the baby was helped by the parent to manage aggressive feelings and experience more depressive concern.

It is not expected that the baby will act as a container for the mother; indeed, this would be seen as a very unhealthy situation. Following Bion (1962b), Emanuel (1984) states, 'The establishment or not of a capacity to think in the infant depends upon the mother's capacity for reverie, that is her capacity to contain and try to understand or think about the infant's primitive communications' (Emanuel, 1984, p. 74), again emphasising the different roles of the mother and the baby. Bion himself wrote:

Reverie is that state of mind which is open to the reception of any 'objects' from the loved object and is therefore capable of reception of the infant's projective identifications whether they are felt by the infant to be good or bad. In short, reverie is a factor of the mother's alpha function.

(Bion, 1962a, p. 36)

Again he emphasised the role of the mother.

The theory of reciprocity, however, involves both mother and baby as active partners. It is fundamental that the mother and the baby are both active in seeking contact with each other. Both partners are active in the relationship.

Secondly, reciprocity is perhaps more observable and concerned with external relationships than is containment, in that reciprocity can be easily observed, as demonstrated by Brazelton (Brazelton et al., 1974) and subsequent researchers. Reciprocity involves the experience of having a manifest effect on the other person, of potency, and of directly observed responsiveness. It involves cooperation between two people. The act of containment is not easy to observe, although the results can be seen, as in the earlier example of Georgie (Reid, 1990), where the containment of Georgie's terror allows him to move from an attachment behaviour of clinging onto the therapist to exploratory behaviour, exploring the room and the toys. It can also be seen in other vignettes described earlier, including that of Besnard et al. (1998): 'Mme Martine arrives with the feeding bottle. She speaks to him reassuringly and lifts him up. Maxime stops crying at once. He immediately relaxes and looks intently at his mother' (p. 53). This is repeated in many clinical accounts in the journals that as a particular emotion is contained, the child is seen to 'move on' in some way. As Trowell (2003) pointed out, perhaps future research on containment could use microanalysis of filmed interactions, especially concentrating on eye movements. Because containment is largely conceptualised as an internal process by psychoanalytic psychotherapists, there has, as far as I am aware, not been any research attempting to describe the observable, behavioural components.

Thirdly, in the literature, the use of the concept of containment usually encompasses negative feelings, whereas descriptions of reciprocity usually concentrate on more positive feelings. Tronick's work, described earlier (Tronick, 1989), on mutual affect regulation does explicitly include 'negative' emotions, but only as a precursor for mutual affect regulation to transform the negative emotion into a positive one, whereas containment focuses on making the negative emotion more manageable, neither removing it nor transforming it into a positive emotion.

Bion used the word 'reciprocity' when writing about containment (Bion, 1970). However, he meant the reciprocal relationship between words and meaning or between memory and remembering, in that a word may contain a meaning and a meaning may contain a word. He did, however, use it in the sense of a reciprocal relationship between people. He referred to 'the fluctuations which make the analyst at one moment the "container" and the analysand the "contained", and at the next reverse the roles' (Bion, 1970, p. 108). This is contrary to the received wisdom for mothers and babies, that the mother should be the container and the infant should be the contained, or the outcome will be detrimental to the infant. The infant should not have to detoxify the paranoid states of the mother. Even though Bion is here referring to adults, because it is the relationship between the analyst and analysand, the way in which he refers to these fluctuations seems more related to Tronick's mutual affect regulation (Tronick et al., 1986). In the quotation above about the analyst and analysand, where both fluctuate between the roles of container and contained, Bion is perhaps bringing together his idea of containment that detoxifies projective identification and the to and fro nature of reciprocity in its everyday linguistic sense, as the rapid interplay between human beings seems to require more than the concept of containment to explain the rapidity and rhythm of human interaction. This sense of containment would be at the microcontainment end of the continuum, linked to mutual affect regulation.

The concept of containment is not the same as the concept of reciprocity, but they are linked, as can be seen above.

Do they take place in the unconscious or conscious mind?

It might be thought that containment is both an intrapsychic and relational concept, whereas reciprocity is relational. However, I think that both require the concepts of projection and introjection, in order to provide a mechanism for the outward communication of an emotion and the inward reception of an emotional communication. Thus, reciprocity is also intrapsychic. Child development theorists tend not to use the concepts of projection and introjection from psychoanalytic theory, but these concepts would provide an explanatory theoretical mechanism within the concept of reciprocity. The concept of reciprocity could use introjection to explain how the baby builds up an expectation of how people will interact and how the baby is able to participate in mutual affect regulation. Were projection to be used to provide an explanatory mechanism within reciprocity, I think it would differ in its intent from its use in the concept of containment. The concept of containment uses the concept of projection to provide a means of communicating emotions as well as a mechanism for getting rid of troublesome emotions, whereas, in reciprocity, the communication of emotions would be the primary purpose of projection.

As a phenomenon, the process of containment may occur predominantly at an unconscious level; however, it can also be consciously facilitated. For example, it is extremely helpful therapeutically to know about the concept of containment, as this can then inform the setting up of a 'containing' situation that will increase the probability of a helpful intervention occurring. For a child psychotherapist, this translates practically into ensuring that sessions begin and end on time and are in the same room for every session, and that substantial notice is given before a holiday. It also informs the emotional stance taken in the sessions, where the therapist orients towards thoughtfulness rather than action in the session, knowing that much of the emotional work in the session will be the containment of powerful emotions and even terror for the child. It can also inform the work of other professionals. For example, a health visitor, instead of attempting to address the concerns of an upset mother in the midst of a busy clinic, by the weighing scales with other mothers present, makes an appointment for a home visit. This seemingly simple action can indicate to the mother that the health visitor has made the time to listen and is also open to listen to her concerns, preparing a 'state of mind' for both the health visitor and mother, and preparing the ground for the potential of a containing interaction. A knowledge of containment also prepares the health visitor for the importance and the impact of emotional communication within the session. Preliminary results suggest that this can be an effective way of working for health visitors (Douglas & Brennan, 2004). Hence, containment is a process that occurs within both the unconscious and the conscious mind, in that it can be utilised consciously.

In everyday life, the phenomenon of reciprocity takes place at an unconscious level. Adults often participate in interactions with infants without conscious thought, altering the tone and level of affect in their voice and waiting for the end of the look-away section of the dance before re-engaging with no conscious knowledge of a look-away cycle existing. This is supported by child development research.

Microanalysis of film has revealed that mother and infant live in a split-second world where the behaviours last for less than half a

second. Each partner responds to the other extremely rapidly, the
time ranging from simultaneous to one-half sec. . . . This rapidity
suggests that, at least for the mother, these split-second adjustments occur partially or fully out of conscious control.

(Beebe & Lachmann, 2002, p. 100)

I suggest that the processes of projection and introjection can be
presumed to underpin reciprocity and that these occur within the
unconscious. However, reciprocity, as well as containment, can be
facilitated through the use of conscious thought. For example, as
mentioned previously, anecdotal evidence within Solihull's Sure Start
project has shown that explaining reciprocity to teenage mothers with
low self-esteem results in their being able to wait for the baby in the
look-away cycle instead of experiencing the look-away as a personal
rejection, thus preventing the chase and dodge sequence from occurring with the resultant disturbances in the relationship between
mother and baby (Beebe & Lachmann, 2002). Implications for the use
of the awareness of reciprocity within psychoanalytic psychotherapy
sessions will be addressed below. However, evidence from the sessions
quoted above indicates that the immediacy and the intense feeling of
being in touch with the other person that can result from reciprocity
perhaps emanates from the unconscious mind. Thus, reciprocity also
takes place within the conscious and unconscious mind.

Is the capacity for containment and reciprocity present in the newborn?

In 1998, Hofacker and Papousek concluded that there was still a lack
of knowledge and understanding about infants' communication in the
mother–infant dyad, 24 years after Brazelton's original paper. It may
be rather premature to try to answer a question about the capacity of
newborns, as, even with the rapid increase in infancy studies, it is often
older infants who have been studied (probably because it has been
easier) rather than newborns and those in the first few days of life,
although this is now beginning to change, with an increased interest in
research on newborns, premature babies and babies not yet born (e.g.,
Hepper, 2005). A brief examination of the two areas of emotional
expression and imitation in infant research, relevant because both are
involved in relationships, show that findings are emerging that include
newborns, although there is a need for more research.

Research on the onset of voluntary communication looked at
intentional smiling in infants from the age of 8–12 months and found

that infants do smile in anticipation of something, and not just as a response to something (Jones & Hong, 2001). Reciprocity would predict voluntary and intentional communication being present earlier, from birth. This has been borne out by recent research. Sullivan and Lewis (2003) reviewed studies that have shown that social smiling peaks between the age of 12 and 14 weeks, but, importantly, they reviewed studies that showed that 'context-appropriate emotional expressions occur in infants from birth or shortly thereafter' (Sullivan & Lewis, 2003, p. 124). New imaging techniques have shown that foetuses smile and cry in the womb from the age of 26 weeks after conception (Campbell, 2004). This research is too new for anyone to have worked out a research paradigm for discovering whether this is 'context-appropriate', although research has shown that foetuses react to noxious stimuli in the womb (Hepper, 2005), so presumably they will react emotionally to different events in the womb.

Research on vocal imitation in two to four-month-old infants (Kokkinaki & Kugiumutzakis, 2000) showed that:

> In early imitative games, as we have hypothesized (Kugiumutza-kis, 1994) and proved (Kokkinaki, 1998), parents and infants share before, during and after imitation two specific kinds of emotion: interest and pleasure. Given that emotions are regarded as motives in human intentional communication, this later finding (Trevarthen, Kokkinaki and Fiamenghi, 1999) provides evidence that infants and parents also share the ability to read each others' motives and intentions.
>
> (Kokkinaki & Kugiumutzakis, 2000, p. 185)

Nagy and Molnar (1994) showed that babies less than two days old could imitate. They also showed that newborns could produce pre-viously imitated gestures while waiting for the experimenter's response.

Kokkinaki (2003) showed that emotional coordination between the infant and parent was evident before, during and after an episode of imitation, either by the infant and parent matching their expression or by attunement. The same occurred in dyads in Crete and in Scotland. Kokkinaki suggested that this showed that the parent and infant were both motivated and that they shared this motivation.

The photographs of Murray and Andrews (2000) show baby Ethan imitating his father. The accompanying text reads:

> He gazes intently at his father, he is concentrated and serious and thoroughly explores John's face. His eyes scan John's features

and he remains totally absorbed for some minutes. John slowly and clearly protrudes his tongue, and Ethan attends closely. Ethan continues to look seriously at his father, and then he begins to move his mouth. Ethan appears to be concentrating completely on his mouth as he frowns and shuts his eyes. Then he looks back at his father as he protrudes his own tongue.

(Murray & Andrews, 2000, p. 28)

The amazing thing about this series of photographs is that Ethan is only 20 minutes old. This shows Ethan engaging in a reciprocal interaction in the first half-hour after birth. It also illustrates the look-away cycle and that it seems to be in that time of turning away from the interaction that processing is occurring in the brain, so that Ethan is then able to carry out a new intentional behaviour.

Fantz and Nevis (1967) showed that newborns liked to look at 3-D objects separate from their own bodies and specifically showed a preference for human faces. This research has been replicated many times. Papousek (1967) observed babies showing pleasure in success and irritation at failure, that is, that they were active learners and took pleasure in learning new things. Panksepp (2000) reviewed the evidence for neurobiological systems underpinning emotions and concluded that these are present from birth (interestingly, Panksepp integrates some of the findings with some of Freud's thinking). DeCasper and Carstens (1981) demonstrated that newborns took a special interest in the human voice and were intentional in seeking responsive company. Babies not only prefer the human voice, but they also show an extraordinary sensitivity to the emotional content of speech (Fernald, 1992; Papousek & Papousek, 1987) and an appreciation of musical features, including rhythm (Trevarthen, 1999), which must be linked to the features of speech and interaction. Nagy and Molnar (1994) worked with babies under two days old. They found that if they waited after a baby had imitated them, the baby would produce the imitation again. The baby's heart rate would speed up as he produced the imitation but then slowed as he waited for a response. They interpreted this as the baby readying himself for interaction and also provoking interaction; that is, the baby intentionally interacted.

While looking at psychoanalytic theory in the light of child development research, I would like to take author's privilege and take a very brief detour from examining containment to examine the concept of primary narcissism, as child development research does have something to contribute to psychodynamic theories. Bion briefly mentioned another psychoanalytic concept, that of primary narcissism: 'emotion

. . . gives reality to objects which are not self and therefore inimical to primary narcissism' (Bion, 1959, p. 108). However, babies seem to seek out objects which are not themselves and wish to interact with the other (DeCaspar and Carstans, 1981; Fantz and Nevis, 1967; Fernald, 1992; Nagy & Molnar, 1994; Papousek & Papousek, 1987), so this does not support the idea of a developmental stage of primary narcissism in infants. I mention this in order to provide another example of how research from another field can be helpful in examining theoretical concepts.

But, back to reciprocity and containment. Most of the research on reciprocity and related theories suggests that the capacity for reciprocity is present from birth (e.g., Trevarthen, 2003). Some psychoanalytic writers on containment suggest that the capacity to contain develops through the experience of being contained: 'The mental equipment and its capacity to metabolise contents develop only gradually' (Williams, 1997). Others infer otherwise. For example, Judy Shuttleworth (1998a) summarised current research on the development of the mind, that the capacity to relate exists

> from birth (or earlier), an innate neurologically-based structure. What human contact, *when it is fully available* [my emphasis] . . . delivers to the infant is an immediate, rather than inferred, awareness of being engaged with another mind. Without this immediate basis, given in experience, the infant would require to slowly construct a theory about the existence of other minds based on inference and prediction. It is just this powerfully generative contact between a developing mind and the immediacy of live experience which Infant Observation attempts to capture.
> (Shuttleworth, 1998a, p. 46)

Shuttleworth was perhaps intimating that a theory of mind is present from birth. Perhaps, of course, both positions are 'true', in the sense of a thesis and antithesis requiring a synthesis, as with the nature/nurture debate; that is, that the ability to contain needs to develop *and* that it is present in some form at birth. The concepts of microcontainment and mutual affect regulation assume that infants can contribute to the containment or mutual affect regulation processes from birth. Some infants may already have the experience of reciprocity or containment in the womb, 'the mating of pre-conception with sense-impressions to produce a conception' (Bion, 1962a).

At this point, it is not possible to say conclusively whether at birth containment precedes reciprocity or vice versa, but the evidence seems to indicate that both are present. My own view is that babies are born with a rudimentary ability for containment, which is at the micro-containment end of the continuum, and which, like everything else, varies between individual babies. This is consonant with Bion's view of a preconception meeting with a realisation to produce a conception (Bion, 1962a), in that as soon as a baby experiences distress and has the experience of being contained, the baby begins to build up the concept of containment. Babies may be born with a more developed capacity for reciprocity, and this, again, varies according to the individual. Some babies are unable to regulate themselves, while others already have some capacity. Most babies have some of the capacities necessary to relate to others 'hard-wired' in their brain so that they can relate from birth (Schore, 1994), or even before birth.

I suggest, therefore, that both containment and reciprocity are present at birth and that there is an interplay between them. When the research is more advanced, it will be interesting to see how both these abilities are affected by the baby's life in the womb. One could already hypothesise that hearing domestic violence and being bathed in the mother's stress hormones in the womb will have an effect on the developing emotional capacity of the child; indeed, a review of the effects of domestic violence in pregnancy, carried out by Jasinski (2004), has outlined the detrimental effects of domestic violence on the developing foetus. Some mothers and fathers already talk to their baby in the womb and interact non-verbally by touching and stroking the part of the baby pushing up against the mother's womb and visible from the outside by the alteration of the curvature of the mother's skin. It would be interesting to discover how this pre-birth interaction affects the infant.

Is containment necessary for reciprocity to occur or vice versa?

The mother–baby interaction is beautifully illustrated in a series of photographs of the moments after baby Ethan's birth (Murray & Andrews, 2000). In the two minutes immediately following his birth, the photographs show his distress at being instantly removed from his mother to have his breathing checked, his mother responding to his distress when he is returned to her by containing him both physically and with her words, and then show Ethan gazing up at her, scanning her face. In this case, containment preceded their reciprocal interaction.

Louise Emanuel's work (Emanuel, 1997) with Sula, a very deprived six-year-old girl who had suffered anoxia at birth and was on the

Child Protection Register, was described earlier. There are several moments in their work together which I think can be described as reciprocity. For instance, early in the therapy, there is a description of a process in the session: 'What followed seemed like a dance between us composed of minute steps and movements' (Emanuel, 1997, p. 290), and this seems very close to a description of the dance of reciprocity. The establishment of reciprocity seemed to be necessary for Sula, before the work could progress. Broadly, in this paper, it seems that the establishment of a reciprocal object preceded that of a containing object.

David Trevatt's work with five-year-old Michael, who had been in foster care and then physically and sexually abused by his foster carers (Trevatt, 1999), as outlined earlier, showed the presence of reciprocity in the sessions. However, in these sessions it seemed that the therapist needed to engage in reciprocal and containing interactions simultaneously. The therapist had to become very active in the session while also containing powerful projections from Michael.

Sue Reid's work with Georgie, two years old and in foster care after suffering emotional abuse, has been described earlier. When he is terrified and clings to her at the beginning of the second session, it seems that she establishes a reciprocal object before a containing one, although the two are intertwined throughout the sessions. The description of a session after two months of therapy, in which the therapist moves from a state of reverie to communicate with him and he repeatedly plays a game which she is able to interpret, seems to show an interplay between reciprocity and containment.

The work of Ann Wells (1997) has been described earlier. She worked with Helen, aged six years, who had been chronically sexually abused and had suffered from many serious illnesses requiring hospital admission. The therapist felt that she had to establish a responsive object ('Mothers by their words and actions provide a patterned context for their baby's sounds and movements. These patterns are sometimes active, sometimes soothing; out of them develops mutual communication and, eventually, language' (Wells, 1997, p. 105)) before she could begin to interpret emotion and the reasons for the emotion. Here it seemed that a responsive object first needed to be established in the therapy before further progress could be made.

The sequence described earlier from Margot Waddell (1998), using an observation by Judy Shuttleworth, showed a mother soothing her shrieking baby so that he was able then to begin the dance of reciprocity with her: 'Then he lay back in his mother's arms and gazed at her face. She smiled and talked to him. He cooed in reply and waved his hands' (Waddell, 1998, p. 29). In this case, containment preceded reciprocity.

The description by Besnard et al. (1998) of an eight-day-old boy, Maxime, with his mother, outlined earlier, showed containment setting the scene for a reciprocal interaction.

> He puckers his face even more, his hands twist, his arms begin to flail about, and he starts to cry. Mme Martine arrives with the feeding bottle. She speaks to him reassuringly and lifts him up. Maxime stops crying at once. He immediately relaxes and looks intently at his mother.
>
> (Besnard et al., 1998, p. 53)

From the evidence, it seems that in some situations containment precedes reciprocity and in other situations reciprocity precedes containment, and in those instances quoted perhaps the presence of one was required before the other. Currently, it would require further work on a wider range of examples to determine the criteria for which situations require which sequence, although one criterion could be the intensity of emotion. That is, if the emotion that is present is very intense, perhaps containment is required before reciprocity can take place. Wolf (2003) pointed out how Bion's infant was a theoretical one, where Bion had to use his speculative imagination to work out his ideas. The original concept of containment implied that the adult modulates the level of affect for the infant. The research seems to show that infants seek emotion. Singh et al. (2002) have shown that one reason why infants prefer 'motherese', the slow sing-song tones used by adults when talking to babies, is the heightened level of emotion expressed in the voice. They found that when the same level of heightened emotion was used in 'normal' speech, the baby equally preferred the two modes of speech. It may be that powerful negative emotion is disliked by the infant, or that it is not the particular emotion, but the level of affect of that emotion that causes discomfort, so that it is the arousal level that is mediated through the other. This links very closely with affect regulation or microcontainment, where I propose that where the level of affect is lower, a rudimentary ability for containment already exists within the infant, who can work together with the mother. However, with a more intense level of affect, the more mature abilities of the mother are required to help the baby contain the emotion.

It probably has not escaped the reader's notice that the examples from therapy sessions largely show reciprocity occurring before containment, whereas the examples from mothers and their babies show containment occurring before reciprocity. I am not sure why this is. One reason could be just coincidence, with a small number of samples. Another could be that the mother–baby interactions are with 'normal' mothers and babies, whereas the therapy sessions are all with children who have been abused. These children have probably not had either containing or reciprocal relationships with their mother (Michael had no such relationship with either his mother or with his substitute carer), and the basic building block of human interaction (reciprocity) may need to be established before work with the emotions can be done.

The presence of a reciprocal relationship may be necessary for containment to function at one end of the spectrum, in that there needs to be an external reciprocal relationship in order for containment to occur in the to and fro of microcontainment. However, from the middle to the macrocontainment end of the spectrum, it may not be necessary for reciprocity to be present, in that it requires the active partner, the 'container', to be only very briefly in tune with the other in order to be able to receive and process the communication and to communicate that to the other. The other may need to be only briefly receptive in order to receive this communication. It is not in the same league as the active, to and fro nature of reciprocity over time. In Brazelton's original paper (Brazelton et al., 1974), the elements of the dance might take 16 seconds to complete. In macrocontainment, it may be that the two psyches are in contact for only milliseconds. There may therefore be a decreasing need for the presence of reciprocity as we travel up the containment continuum, from microcontainment, which would need reciprocity, to containment, which may or may not need a reciprocal relationship, to macrocontainment which can occur without the pattern of a reciprocal relationship. These conclusions are extremely tentative, but I include them in order to identify further areas for research.

In therapy sessions, for some children, perhaps the establishment of an interaction with a responsive object needs to occur in the sessions before containment can be fully experienced by the child, but for other children the reverse may be true. For example, establishing a reciprocal object first may be more important for children who have a depressive mother, whereas for hyperactive children it may be more important to establish a containing object first.

The elaboration of the relationship between the two concepts may have implications, therefore, for therapeutic work; for instance, in those therapeutic sessions where a responsive object needs to be established before a containing object. The evidence from the sessions examined earlier suggests that the push is by the child to engage a responsive object. It is the child who initiates this, forcing the therapist to interact (or not). This is different from the modification of technique described by Alvarez (1999) with autistic children, in which the therapist seeks out the faintest sign of a wish to interact in the child. In amplified reciprocity, it is the therapist who initiates the contact. In reciprocity in the therapy sessions, it seems to be the child who elicits the reciprocal interaction from the therapist, especially in the case of therapists who do not consider reciprocity as part of their work, and so would not be using it or looking for it in their sessions. In other words, currently, the push would need to be from the child to get the therapist to work with them in a reciprocal interaction. It seems that after the responsive object, the therapist, has been established, the more usual Kleinian work of containment and interpretation within the transference can be carried out. This is not necessary for every child, as some children in therapy already have a responsive object and can move rapidly into the usual Kleinian therapeutic work.

Perhaps this is how the great debate arose between the thesis of Melanie Klein and the antithesis of Anna Freud, where Klein went straight into interpreting the child's deepest anxieties (using containment, although it was not called that then), and Anna Freud made a link with the child first through educational activities (perhaps using an interaction that was more based on reciprocity, although it was not called that then). Perhaps the synthesis is that a version of both is needed, and for some children it is important to establish a responsive object before establishing a containing object, or it needs to be done in tandem.

Communication and language

Both containment and reciprocity are involved in communication and language (Lock, 1978) and a sense of self (Stern, 1985). Segal (1957) wrote about the relationship of containment to the learning of meaningful speech. This is one aspect of communication. Reciprocity is another. To communicate requires turn taking, the rhythm of speech, the rhythm between people alternately speaking and listening. Reciprocity involves reaching out, the rhythm of contact, the rules of contact. Symbolic thought arises out of the 'immediacy of the two-person relationship of primary intersubjectivity' (Shuttleworth, 1998a, p. 47).

Containment also involves communication by projection of an internal state, but Bion implies that the communication is based on this, not on a seeking of contact with another in a reciprocal state. Containment gives meaning to internal states, processes these into thoughts, and translates thoughts into words. It lends meaning to experience, and this is the beginning of language. Containment is more concerned with the internal world, while reciprocity is at the boundary between the internal and external worlds. Thus, both containment and reciprocity are involved in the genesis of language development.

In the previous chapter, I outlined the relationship between the different degrees of reciprocity and the different degrees of containment. In this chapter, I have outlined some of the similarities and differences between the two concepts. Firstly, the concept of containment and the concept of reciprocity differ in the roles they allocate to the mother and the baby. Secondly, reciprocity is perhaps more observable and concerned with external relationships than is containment. Thirdly, in the literature, the use of the concept of containment usually encompasses negative feelings, whereas descriptions of reciprocity usually concentrate on more positive feelings. Fourthly, the unconscious and the conscious mind are involved in both phenomena, although the unconscious mind is perhaps predominant in containment. I propose that the processes of projection and introjection can be presumed to underpin reciprocity and these occur within the unconscious. However, reciprocity, as well as containment, can be facilitated by conscious thought. Fifthly, I suggest that a capacity exists in the infant from birth to participate in a reciprocal interaction and to contain emotions at the microcontainment level, though the capacity varies from infant to infant. Sixthly, from the evidence, it seems that in some situations containment precedes reciprocity, and in other situations reciprocity precedes containment. The therapeutic implications of this are that, for some children, perhaps establishing a reciprocal object first needs to occur in the sessions before containment can be experienced by the child, but for other children the reverse may be true. I also suggest that it may be possible to define differentially when one is required rather than the other, so that children who have experienced a non-responsive mother may need a responsive object established in the first instance. Seventhly, both phenomena are involved in the genesis and development of communication and language.

9 How does reciprocity link to therapeutic theory and technique?

In Chapter 5, we looked at examples of reciprocity occurring within the accounts of psychoanalytic work. This chapter will examine how reciprocity relates to current therapeutic technique.

Is reciprocity in therapeutic sessions just 'acting out'?

When therapists find that they have carried out an impulsive act within a session, they usually examine whether they were 'acting out'. Laplanche and Pontalis (1988) characterised acting out as a compulsion to repeat, rather than to understand. The other characteristics are that the act is impulsive, a radical departure from usual behaviour, usually aggressive and always 'ill-motivated'. The acts described in this paper are often characterised by the therapists themselves as not being their usual behaviour. They do seem to be impulsive. However, they do not have the main feature of a compulsion to repeat rather than understand, in that all the therapists cited have the sense of something that is *new* occurring for both partners. They can be sudden, can happen without conscious thought, and are presumably rooted in the primitive impulse to connect with another. However, they are not aggressive and not ill-motivated. These moments appear to help therapists' thinking and the growth of their understanding of the transference and counter-transference relationships. Examples of reciprocity within sessions therefore do not have the characteristics of acting out.

Reciprocity and therapeutic technique with adults

So far, I have considered therapeutic work with children and adults in their role as parents. However, a knowledge of reciprocity may also be useful in therapeutic work with adults. It is possible that for the difficult-to-reach adult patients described by Joseph (1975) it has perhaps been the failure to establish a responsive object that led to both the usual interpretative work having little effect and the fact that they are difficult to reach. Some adults may suffer from chronic dissociation, rather than a more temporary reaction to trauma, and may require a different technique. Joseph pointed out that in the difficult-to-reach adults the potentially responsive part is split off and that the main aim of the analysis is to get in touch with them. She has modified her technique, in that the meaning of the words that the patient uses is secondary to everything else involved in the communication: what Meltzer might call the 'temperature' (1976), as discussed below. Joseph emphasised the necessity to keep interpretations immediate, direct and in contact with the here-and-now in the session. This may be a link with reciprocity, together with her intent to concentrate on the non-verbal aspects of the verbal communication. Incorporating more thought about reciprocity might be part of the technique for such adults.

Temperature and distance

Temperature and distance were discussed by Meltzer (1976). He considered emotional temperature and distance, that is, the level of intensity of affect.

> Its elements would be the ordinary ones of music: tone, rhythm, key, volume and timbre. By modulating these musical elements we can control the emotionality of the voice and thus what I mean by personal communication. This in turn has an impact on the emotional atmosphere of the consulting room and the reverberation between patient and analyst, variously heightening or dampening this atmosphere.
>
> (Meltzer, 1976, p. 63)

Meltzer was thinking about general aspects of the relationship between therapist and patient, related to the level of intensity of affect and to what seems bearable at any given moment, so it is interesting that he noticed elements of reciprocity. He indirectly linked temperature to reciprocity through rhythm. The rhythm of interaction and the musicality of reciprocity have been especially emphasised by Trevarthen (e.g. Trevarthen, 1999). I think Meltzer also refers to reciprocity when he mentions the 'reverberation' between the therapist and patient, as this could be the microsecond-to-microsecond adjustment within reciprocity (Beebe & Lachmann, 2002). It is interesting to note that he would be referring to therapy with adults, with the adult lying on a couch with his back to the therapist; hence the emphasis on the voice and the qualities of the voice, as the usual interactive, visual mode is not available in this situation. (This would have links to a mother with a blind baby, where the voice would be one of the main modes of communication in reciprocity.) Meltzer was therefore struck by some of the elements in the therapeutic relationship, which, even though they are not named as such, are part of reciprocity. Here, the elements are related to mutual affect regulation and microcontainment. Although Meltzer wrote, '*we* can control' (my emphasis), I think he was referring to a controlling action by therapists rather than an activity controlled by both therapist and patient. In the light of the links between the temperature and distance of a therapeutic interaction and reciprocity, it may therefore be helpful to consider reciprocity when considering the relationship between the therapist and the patient.

Primary disappointment

Reciprocity may be especially important for children who have dead, depressed or unresponsive internal objects, related to a primary disappointment (Emanuel, 1984). Ricky Emanuel describes how a primary disappointment occurs when 'there is a failure of the parental object to meet his innate expectations. This includes the infant's expectations of a containing object that can "think" about him' (p. 10). Containment then becomes the mechanism through which the internal objects are modified and a thinking object is established. However, I suggest that there is also an innate expectation of a responsive object. As mentioned before, most infants try from birth to interact with their external objects and in visual experiments prefer anything resembling a face (Stern, 1985). If these early processes are interrupted by neglect, deprivation or the presence of an unresponsive object, the result may equally be a primary disappointment. This may also be the case for inappropriately responding objects, such as a schizophrenic mother. It may be that for these patients it would be helpful to think about reciprocity and a responsive object. As already noted, it may be that reciprocity can also be considered where adult patients have a failure in an internal responsive object.

A transference activity?

Betty Joseph (1985) described the therapeutic experience as a total transference activity, where everything, from moment to moment, is part of the transference and counter-transference. Reciprocity also occurs within this milieu, so, within this definition, reciprocity becomes part of the transference activity. Although it may result in a non-verbal act or a particular type of verbal communication, such as singing, both are informed by the therapist's intuitive understanding of the transference/counter-transference relationship. Currently, these are 'intuitive' because, at present, reciprocity is not usually consciously thought about within sessions. At the present time, child psycho-therapists are familiar with the concept of containment, because it is made explicit at many points during the training, but reciprocity is mentioned in the preclinical training only in the context of child development research and is not related to clinical work. This total transference activity links to Meltzer's consideration of temperature and distance. All the information contributes to the counter-transference. Being aware of how in tune one is or is not in the interaction is also part of the transference/counter-transference and can be informed by an awareness of reciprocity.

An interpretative activity?

Interpretation is a core activity within psychoanalytic psychotherapy sessions. It is therefore pertinent to consider whether reciprocity is an interpretive activity. Symington (1986) described three types of interpretation: keeping the conversation going, exploratory guesses and interpretation proper. Laplanche and Pontalis (1988) defined interpretation as a 'procedure which, by means of analytic investi-gation, brings out the latent meaning in what the subject says and does. Interpretation reveals the modes of defensive conflict and its ultimate aim is to identify the wish that is expressed by every product of the unconscious' (p. 227). Some of the clinical examples involve verbal activity as part of them, as when Bartram is counting to three in time with the child preparing to jump off the table. This is not interpretation. Sue Reid's example of calming Georgie began to turn into a description of his feelings, and this may be the precursor of an interpretation, putting feelings into words and feeding them back, but her activity at the time seems more linked to containment than reciprocity. It may be that reciprocity is not an interpretative activity but, in some cases, a precondition of helpful interpretative activity. It may be helpful when working with children who are unable to respond to interpretations, where a responsive object needs to be established first. As discussed before, this may be especially relevant to children with a primary disappointment (Emanuel, 1984), where the primary carer has been unresponsive, for whatever reason. Reciprocity does not appear to be an interpretative activity, but it could be considered to be a pre-interpretative activity, preparing the ground for interpretation.

Reciprocity and intuition

Finally, I would like to consider the relationship of reciprocity to intuition. Intuition is sometimes used in a particular way in psychoanalytic psychotherapy. Britton (1998) refers to the role of intuition in analysis, where the intuition of the analyst is used to remain close to the thinking of the patient in order to select what needs to be attended to in the interpretation. From the examples of reciprocity discovered in psychoanalytic material, one aspect of some reciprocal interactions is that they may be seen as intuitive, according to a dictionary definition of the usual use of the term. They are immediate, intense and at a deep level of feeling and contact. *Collins Concise English Dictionary* defines intuition as 'knowledge or perception not gained by reasoning or intelligence', and the immediacy of the reciprocity in these examples would meet this definition. Intuition in the examples in this book is probably related to something 'pre-thinking': that is, attending to a feeling. Reciprocity occurring in therapy is currently intuitive, because it has not been named within the process of therapy and so is not specifically attended to, and this concurs with the dictionary definition. However, it would be interesting to integrate a knowledge of reciprocity into the milieu of therapy. Intuition could then be used in the sense of Britton's definition. The intuition of the therapist would then be used to remain close not only to the thinking of the patient but also to the interactive relationship with the patient (as, I think, probably already happens in many sessions) and to attend to reciprocity as part of the work of interpretation.

This chapter has outlined some of the considerations of reciprocity in therapeutic situations. The most obvious is the application of reciprocity as amplified reciprocity, as used by Alvarez and others (Alvarez, 1999) in an attempt to reach 'hard-to-reach' children. The concept of acting out was examined to consider whether reciprocity could be considered as an acting-out activity. However, the conclusion was drawn that reciprocity in itself is not an example of acting out. A brief outline was given as to why a knowledge of reciprocity might be useful in therapeutic work with adults. Links were made between Meltzer's ideas (Meltzer, 1976) of temperature and distance in therapeutic sessions and reciprocity; hence, we may assume that a knowledge of reciprocity might be helpful in understanding the relationship between the patient and the therapist. Emanuel's work (Emanuel, 1984) on primary disappointments was linked to reciprocity; that is, to the idea that reciprocity may be especially important for children who have dead, depressed or unresponsive internal objects, related to a primary disappointment. Reciprocity was seen as part of the transference activity in the therapeutic session, from Betty Joseph's description (Joseph, 1985) of the therapeutic experience as a total transference activity, where everything, from moment to moment, is part of the transference and counter-transference. Consideration was given as to whether reciprocity could be seen as part of interpretative activity, starting with the work of Symington (1986). The conclusion was drawn that reciprocity is not an interpretative activity, but may be, in some cases, a precondition of helpful interpretative activity.

The idea of intuition in therapy, as defined by Britton (1998), was examined. Reciprocity could be used by the intuition of the therapist to pay attention to the interactive relationship with the patient. An explicit use of reciprocity may have a place with children from certain backgrounds and with certain characteristics. It can be used in transference/counter-transference, to illuminate the relationship, to add to awareness of the temperature and distance in the session, and to set the scene for interpretative activity.

10 How does attachment relate to containment and reciprocity?

Attachment (Bowlby, 1969, 1988) is an influential theory, differing from containment and reciprocity because it arises from both traditions, in part from the psychoanalytic tradition and in part from a child development perspective. All three ideas, attachment, containment and reciprocity, begin by saying something deceptively simple about the human condition, but all three have generated layers of meaning and complexity.

The vignettes quoted in this book do not show the relationship between attachment and containment and reciprocity. The vignettes chosen all reflect a few moments in time, whereas an attachment is built up over time. However, I propose that two of the main building blocks used to create the quality of an attachment are containment and reciprocity and that this can be demonstrated by taking a look at a particular research study by Beebe and at descriptions of interventions said to be based on attachment theory. It is important to emphasise that I am not proposing that containment and reciprocity underpin attachment itself, as, theoretically, attachment is construed as an innate, biological necessity developed through evolutionary processes to promote survival of the individual. However, the quality of attachment varies between individuals, as has been shown by Ainsworth et al. (1978) and in many subsequent studies described by Cassidy and Shaver (1999). The *quality* of the attachment is mediated through other processes, and I am proposing that two of the main processes are containment and reciprocity.

The theory of attachment has developed over time (Fonagy, 2001). The early definition concentrated on the goal of attachment behaviour as being the seeking of proximity, so that the absence of the attachment figure generated the biological need, while the presence of the attachment figure turned it off (Bowlby, 1969). In 1973, Bowlby refined the goal of attachment behaviour as maintaining the availability of the caregiver, which included the accessibility and responsiveness of the caregiver and the role of appraisal by the infant. This led to Bowlby's proposing the existence of an internal working model of the expected availability of the caregiver, together with a working model of the self. In 1977, Sroufe and Waters modified this so that the goal was 'felt security' rather than the actual distance between the child and caregiver or only the actual behaviour of the attachment figure. This left room for intrapsychic mechanisms such as fantasy, projection and introjection, as well as internal representations in both the infant and the parent.

Infants' attachment behaviours were shown to fall into four broad patterns of behaviour. Ainsworth et al. (1978) developed the 'Strange Situation' with infants aged one and two years. This involves the parent leaving the room twice, in rather an unpredictable manner, although within a timed laboratory procedure. There are eight episodes within this strange situation. During episode 1, lasting one minute, the infant and parent are introduced to the room. During episode 2, lasting three minutes, the infant settles in and explores, with the parent assisting only when necessary. During episode 3, lasting three minutes, a stranger enters the room and plays with the infant during the final minute. During episode 4, lasting three minutes, the parent leaves the room, leaving the infant with the stranger. During episode 5, lasting three minutes, the parent returns and the stranger leaves. During episode 6, lasting three minutes, the parent leaves the room again, this time leaving the infant alone. During episode 7, lasting three minutes, the stranger enters the room again, interacting as necessary. During episode 8, lasting three minutes, the parent returns and the stranger leaves. The focus of interest is not on how the infant reacts when the parent leaves, but rather on how the infant acts when the parent returns. The infant's behaviour during these reunions was coded and categorised into one of, initially, three attachment patterns, but is now coded into four. The three patterns are securely attached, avoidant and resistant. The fourth pattern was amplified by Main and Solomon (1986) and is classified as disorganised.

The secure infant either greets the parent or, conversely, clearly shows the parent that he is upset, seeks comfort and is soon comforted by the parent. The avoidant infant avoids the parent on reunion and tends to concentrate on the toys. If he is picked up, he may stiffen or lean away. The resistant infant alternates between trying to contact the parent and rejecting the parent, or, conversely, he may be too upset or passive to make any contact with the parent. The result is that the avoidant and the resistant infants fail to be comforted by the parent, unlike the secure group. In her original study in 1978, Ainsworth used 106 infant–parent dyads, but studied a further 23 dyads in their home situation. She found that the dyads' behaviour at home corroborated the laboratory findings.

The three categories of secure, avoidant and resistant attachments are all examples of organised attachment. There is a definite pattern of behaviour exhibited by the infant. In contrast, however, Main and Solomon (1986) described a fourth category of attachment in which there is no discernible pattern. The infant may freeze, show fear of the parent, or seem confused or disorientated. This behaviour is coded as a disorganised attachment. Subsequent observations of infants in this category suggest that many infants who have been maltreated display these behaviours (Solomon & George, 1999), although infants with a neurological vulnerability may also have a disorganised attachment (Spangler et al., 1996).

An infant displays a particular attachment pattern towards a particular adult. Thus, although a meta-analysis of studies has shown a small trend towards a similar attachment pattern to both parents (van Ijzendoorn & De Wolff, 1997), studies tend to show that infants have different attachment patterns towards different carers (Howes, 1999). The importance of van Ijzendoorn and De Wolff's findings, taken together with that of Howes, is what clinicians have long known, that the effects of a poor-quality attachment relationship with one parent can be mitigated to some extent by a good-quality attachment relationship with the other parent, grandparent or some other adult carer who is in frequent contact with the child. This is recognised by the excellent publication by the UK Department for Education and Skills (2001), which lists risk and resilience factors for children. One of the resilience factors is to have a good attachment relationship with at least one adult. Anecdotally, many workers have the experience of seeing a baby with an emotionally unavailable mother (unavailable perhaps through her own mental health difficulties, preoccupation with domestic violence, substance abuse difficulties, alcohol abuse, etc.), where the baby and the mother are not making eye contact and there is little sign of the dance of reciprocity. Then, when the worker tries to engage the baby, the baby makes eye contact, his eyes brighten, and he begins to vocalise. The baby has not given up. Sometimes this may be because of the qualities of the baby, that he is innately a very sociable and persistent baby, but sometimes it may be that the baby has had frequent experience of a rewarding reciprocal relationship with another. It also follows, unfortunately, that if such a mother is alone and isolated, there will be little chance of the baby's having an alternative experience.

Interestingly, I think that the list of risk factors for children in this publication supports my hypothesis that containment and reciprocity are the building blocks underpinning the attachment relationship, that is, that they can all be seen as interfering with the adults' ability either to participate successfully in the second-to-second reciprocal relationship with their child or to be mindfully and emotionally present enough to help their child through containment. The risk factors in the family are overt parental conflict; family breakdown; inconsistent or unclear discipline; hostile or rejecting relationships; failure to adapt to a child's changing needs; physical, sexual or emotional abuse; parental psychiatric illness, criminality, alcoholism or personality disorder; and death or loss. However, I think that inconsistent or unclear discipline and failure to adapt to a child's changing needs are the result of a parent's not being mindfully present, rather than the cause.

The effects of the availability or not of the mother within an attachment relationship also link with Murray's findings (Murray, 1991), discussed earlier. She demonstrated that, for postnatally depressed mothers, the predictive factors for a negative impact on the development of the infant were neither the length nor severity of the postnatal depression, but the degree to which the mother was immersed within her own experience; that is, her being not available to her child. This means that the mother's ability to be in a containing and/or reciprocal relationship with her child was severely compromised. Again, I propose that this is further evidence that reciprocity and containment are core concepts for understanding the processes through which parents help their child develop, including the quality of the attachment relationship. And thus, they are core concepts for devising interventions to help parents help their children.

However, to return to the 'Strange Situation' and the categories of attachment, the gift of the Strange Situation was that it gave attachment theory an experimental method that generated a great deal of research. This, together with Bowlby's work for WHO (Bowlby, 1951), contributed to the spread of attachment theory around the world. For instance, an Internet search using Google and the key words 'attachment theory' yielded 11,400,000 citations. The differences are interesting between the spread and general knowledge about attachment and the much smaller knowledge community of containment and about reciprocity.

Attachment theory is, however, a descriptive theory, providing descriptive categories for types of attachment. The interpersonal and intrapersonal mechanisms underpinning attachment remain to be detailed. In my view, attachment itself does not promote clinical intervention, because it does not describe the mechanisms through which it can be altered. It describes the conditions necessary for attachment to take place, so that it does have implications for 'environmental' interventions. For paediatric units, this means that parents are allowed to stay and can visit at any time; for midwifery units, that the mother and baby meet together immediately after birth; for adoption, that babies are not handed between different caretakers before being permanently adopted and are not left in hospital with multiple carers; for looked-after children, that they do not have multiple placements; and for nurseries, that children are not subjected to a fast turnover of multiple carers who are reluctant to relate.

An example of how attachment does not suggest a clinical intervention is as follows. In child protection cases, professionals are often asked to give a judgement on the quality of the attachment between the parent and child, and there are standardised tests to assist with this. However, having assisted with the report on the nature and quality of the attachment, attachment theory itself is not able to determine how the attachment between that particular adult and child could be facilitated, because it does not describe the interpersonal and intrapersonal mechanisms through which an attachment is mediated.

From her home observations, Ainsworth suggested that there were differences in four interrelated variables between the mothers of secure, avoidant and resistant infants. These were sensitivity (responding promptly and appropriately to the infant's signals), acceptance, cooperation and psychological accessibility. Sensitivity as a variable has been of central importance in the attachment literature. A meta-analysis of relevant research studies has shown that parental sensitivity is one factor in the development of a secure attachment, but not the exclusive factor (De Wolff & van Ijzendoorn, 1997). However, I think that these variables are not sufficiently worked out to be of much help in work focusing on changing the quality of an attachment. I think that reciprocity relates to sensitivity and containment relates to psychological accessibility, and that both the concepts of containment and reciprocity have a contribution to make in thinking about the mediating variables in the development of the quality of attachment because both already have a large body of thought, literature and, in the case of reciprocity, research. I will show later that reciprocity and its related theories of attunement, intersubjectivity and mutual affect regulation are now being explicitly used in an attachment-based intervention (Marvin et al., 2002).

Attachment and containment

However, I am first going to consider attachment theory and containment. Williams (1998) makes a link between attachment theory and psychoanalytic theory by suggesting that Main's category of disorganised attachment (Main & Solomon, 1986) is related to children having parents who have had traumatic events in their lives and who project anxiety rather than contain it. Further attachment research has shown that parents who have failed to process their traumatic past pass it on to their children. The determinant of whether a parent's traumatic past affects the next generation is not the trauma itself, but whether the trauma was processed. Thus, there is a strong correlation between parents who have had a traumatic past together with a realistic relationship with their past, and their child having a secure attachment. These parents neither demonise nor idealise their past, as demonstrated by the coherence of the story they are able to tell about it. Main and Goldwyn (1984a) began this research, using the Adult Attachment Interview (AAI) (Main & Goldwyn, 1984b), which comprises a semistructured interview using 18 questions and lasts about an hour. Examples of the questions are as follows:

- Could you give me five adjectives or phrases to describe your relationship with your mother/father during childhood? I'll write them down and when we have all five I'll ask you to tell me what memories or experiences led you to choose each one.
- Did you experience the loss of a parent or other close loved one as a child, or in adulthood?

The questions have been designed to discover the adult's internal working model, the representation of that individual's attachment system, a secure attachment being where the individual can use an attachment figure as a secure base in times of trouble.

The four classifications are autonomous, dismissing, preoccupied and unresolved/disorganised. These link to the infant classifications: autonomous to secure, dismissing to avoidant, preoccupied to resistant and unresolved/disorganised to disorganised. Interviewees are judged as having a secure or autonomous attachment if they have a balanced view of early relationships and value attachment relationships; if they have a consistent evaluation of their attachment experiences even if the experiences tended to be negative; and if they can describe experiences in a coherent manner, so that answers to the above question about five adjectives contain corroborating experiences. Someone who says that his or her mother was loving, wonderful and caring but is unable to recall any memories of the mother being loving, wonderful and caring would probably not be classified as autonomous. Adults with a dismissing classification are not coherent, tend to be very brief in their descriptions, and dismiss attachment relationships. Preoccupied adults are also not coherent, but, in contrast to the dismissing adults, tend to produce very long descriptions, are often angry, fearful or passive, and are preoccupied with past attachment relationships. The unresolved/disorganised adults show more incoherence in their narrative. They report trauma and loss but are confused and disorganised in the way in which they are able to talk about it, often showing lapses of reason.

The scoring system for these classifications was developed by Main and Goldwyn by examining the interview transcripts of 44 parents whose infants' attachment status had already been classified by the Strange Situation. They found that autonomous adults tended to have secure infants; dismissing adults, avoidant infants; preoccupied adults, resistant infants; and disorganised adults, disorganised infants.

Main and Goldwyn's work has generated further studies, so that van Ijzendoorn (1995) was able to carry out a meta-analysis of the 14 studies then available, covering 854 dyads, which corroborated the initial finding. The study also showed that the correlation held whether the AAI had been carried out with the parent after the birth of the child or before. An example of a predictive study in which the AAI study was carried out before the birth of the child and then predicted the Strange Situation classification of the child is that of Peter Fonagy and the Steeles (Fonagy, Steele & Steele, 1991). The AAI was carried out with 96 mothers before the birth of their children. When the children were 12 months old, the Strange Situation was carried out. They found that secure mothers tended to have secure children and insecure mothers tended to have insecure children, with 75 per cent predictability. Interestingly, Benoit and Parker (1994) carried out a study across three generations, finding that secure grandmothers tended to have secure daughters, who tended to have secure children.

The concept of containment provides a theoretical mechanism through which this transmission or non-transmission of trauma can be explained, in that it is parents who have themselves contained their experience who can then pass on the experience of having a containing object to their own children, rather than passing on an undigested lump of trauma and the experience of not having the capacity to contain the experience.

The concept of containment also provides the theoretical mechanism through which the development of a secure attachment can be explained. Containment posits that feelings can be felt and can be coped with. The secure infant, upon the parent's returning, is able to be angry or upset and show it, but is soon comforted by the parent. He has learned from and has experience of the parent helping him with these strong emotions. The containment provided by the parent enables him to calm down and resume the exciting exploration of the world. The mechanism for this was shown previously in the description by Sue Reid of her interaction with Georgie (Reid, 1990). She described how she managed to help him with his terror so that he was then able to explore.

> The smallest movement of my body, my face or even my eyes caused him to cry out in terror . . . I manage to stand almost perfectly still and respond by humming to him. Over minutes his body relaxes its grip and when the time feels right, I add words to the hum. It becomes a lullaby in which I use his name and sing of his fear. After more time passes he gets down and moves around the room and to his toy box.
>
> (Reid, 1990, p. 3)

This is the paradox of Bowlby's 'secure base', in that we need a secure base in order to have the capacity to make the most of our epistemological instinct and then to explore, be curious and learn.

However, for both the avoidant infant and the resistant infant, the mechanism of containment has been compromised. The avoidant infant avoids the parent on reunion and tends to concentrate on the toys. If he is picked up, he may stiffen or lean away. This may mean that the infant has learned that the parent has been of no help in coping with upset and anger and has learned to stifle these feelings, distracting himself instead and actively rejecting the parent. The resistant infant alternates between trying to contact the parent and rejecting the parent, or, conversely, he may be too upset or passive to make any contact with the parent. This may mean that the infant has had a very inconsistent experience of containment and feels that the parent cannot be relied upon to provide a containing experience. There is also the interplay to consider between the infant's capacities and the parent's capacities, in that the temperament of the infant may affect his interaction with the parent. This research has been reviewed by Vaughn and Bost (1999). I like one of their interpretations: 'It may be that when a parent's economic, social, and/or psychological resources are strained, an irritable or otherwise difficult infant elicits a less than optimal caregiving, which in turn potentiates the assembly of an insecure attachment' (Vaughn & Bost, 1999, p. 20). However, their overall conclusion is that 'the existing data do not support any strong conclusion, save that attachment and temperament domains are related (to a modest degree) but clearly not isomorphic' (Vaughn & Bost, 1999, p. 21). This conclusion is supported by the theoretical aspects of containment, in that psychoanalytic theory has always incorporated an understanding of the different capacities of different individuals, so that parents differ in their capacity to contain and infants differ in their need for and capacity to respond to the parent. Because I think that infants already have a rudimentary capacity for containment or mutual affect regulation at birth, I would add that infants may differ in this capacity too.

Thus, the concept of containment can provide the theoretical mechanism to explain how a secure attachment is created. It explains why some parents do not transmit their trauma to the next generation, the transmission of which affects the quality of attachment. It can also be used as part of the explanatory mechanism for how, in the day-to-day interaction between a child and his parent, in the many separations and reunions they experience, the parent's ability to contain the infant's upset and anger underpins how the child participates in a Strange Situation reunion.

Attachment and reciprocity

Reciprocity can also be seen as a building block in the quality of an attachment. Beebe and Lachmann (2002) describe a number of their studies examining mother–infant and stranger–infant dialogues, using time-series analysis to examine the vocal rhythms between the dyads, which is part of reciprocity. Beebe's observations are based on time, because infants can recognise time intervals of only fractions of a second from birth (Lewkowicz, 1989). 'Our study of the interpersonal timing of mother–infant interaction rests on this perceptual ability of infants to time the durations of their own and their partners' sounds and silences' (Beebe & Lachmann, 2002, p. 100). The work of Beebe and her colleagues, in microanalysing filmed interactions between infants and others, shows that 'mother and infant live in a split-second world' (Beebe & Lachmann, 2002, p. 100). Interestingly, because the time of a phase of interaction can be so short and the switching between phases so rapid, Beebe suggests that most of the adjustments to the other must occur mostly out of conscious control. This concurs with most of our daily experience, where we are constantly modulating our interaction with another, but are not generally aware of the microsecond phases of the interaction. It also describes what we observe in supermarkets, cafés and post office queues; anywhere where we see mothers or fathers interacting naturally with their baby.

One study (Jaffe et al., 2001) analysed the audiotapes of vocal interactions at home and in the laboratory between four-month-old infants and their mothers, and between the same infants and strangers (female postgraduate students). Measurements were made of the duration of vocalisations, pauses and switching pauses where the turn passed from one to the other. The analysis showed that the interactions were co-regulated for these four-month-old infants. This in itself is not a startling finding and serves to support the evidence that reciprocal interactions can be demonstrated between infants and adults. However, the research went much further. The authors found that 'these indices of temporal coordination of mother–infant and stranger–infant vocal dialogue at four months predicted infant attachment and cognition at one year'. That is, the quality of attachment of the infant at one year of age could be predicted from the type of reciprocal interaction at four months of age. I suggest that this demonstrates that reciprocity is one of the building blocks underpinning the quality of an attachment.

Anecdotally, clinicians have reported that some mothers seem very tuned into their baby early on, but then the relationship seems to deteriorate. The findings of Jaffe et al. provide one explanation. Chapple (1970) suggested that good communication requires high interpersonal coordination. Gottman (1981) suggested the opposite, that high interpersonal coordination is pathological. Warner et al. (1987) suggested that a midrange of interpersonal coordination was best. Jaffe et al. suggest that all of the above are correct depending on the situation. The highly coordinated mother–infant dyad correlated with a disorganised attachment; 'in the prediction of attachment, very high coordination is seen as an index of vigilance, overmonitoring or wariness. Very high coordination may be an adaptive attempt to counteract some discoordination in the interaction' (Beebe & Lachmann, 2002, p. 103). This predicted a disorganised attachment. There was no fluidity in the interaction, between attending and sort of attending, as happens in everyday life. There would be little of the usual process of rupture and repair, which is so essential for learning about hope, optimism and making up after a disagreement. The mother seemed fixed in this pattern of high coordination. 'High coordination in attachment can be interpreted as an attempt to cope with difficulty by making the interaction more predictable' (Beebe & Lachmann, 2002, p. 102).

To complicate the picture, high coordination was sometimes found to be predictive of good things, but only when it happened with the stranger. When the infant at four months old and the stranger had high coordination, this predicted a high cognitive development score when the infant was 12 months old. This may be because the response to novelty is an indicator of intelligence, linking to our curiosity and wish to learn. High coordination in this situation may be a sign of good information processing together with a willingness to learn.

Midrange scores with the mother were found to be optimal in terms of predicting a secure attachment. Each personality significantly affected the other's patterns as they adjusted to each other in this range, so more fluidity and adjustment were possible, and more uncertainty could be present and be coped with.

Midrange scores with the stranger also predicted a secure attachment, but it was also possible to predict the other two categories of attachment, avoidant and resistant, by examining how the infant was with the stranger and vice versa: 'high stranger coordination with infant (but not vice versa) predicted anxious-resistant attachment; low infant coordination with stranger (but not vice versa) predicted avoidant infant attachment' (Beebe & Lachmann, 2002, p. 102).

From these results, it may be possible to draw a link with mutual affect regulation and containment. Beebe, Lachmann, Jaffe and their colleagues suggest that where there is high tracking between the mother and infant, predicting a disorganised attachment, there is excessive monitoring of interactive regulation at the expense of self-regulation. Where there is low tracking between the mother and infant, predicting an insecure attachment, there is a preoccupation with self-regulation at the expense of interactive regulation. That is, where there is excessive monitoring of interactive regulation, the mother is hypervigilant and the infant has also become hypervigilant. As suggested earlier, the mother may be trying to make the inter-action more predictable, for many reasons. However, this pattern of interaction tends to result in an insecure attachment. In terms of containment, one could hypothesise that the regulation of arousal, affect or anxiety for the infant, but also probably for the mother, does not occur within this system. My prediction would be that measurements of anxiety in both the baby and the mother would be high and that the interaction would not serve to lower anxiety levels, unlike in the midrange of coordination, where the state of mind of the mother would allow for flexibility of interaction and for containment within that.

To return to the situation where there is a preoccupation with self-regulation at the expense of interactive regulation, there is evidence from other sources to support this description. Beebe and Lachmann cite Tronick's (1989) work with postnatally depressed mothers and their infants, where he described infants who became preoccupied with their own self-regulation, in the face of continual failures in rupture and repair. They would use many mechanisms to self-soothe: rocking, touching themselves, turning away, and mouthing themselves or objects. I would also add the work of Murray (1991), which I described earlier. Again, with mothers with postnatal depression, Murray showed that a poor outcome for the infant was not the length or severity of the depression but the degree to which the mother was self-preoccupied. That is, in dyads where the mother was over-preoccupied with herself and not available to her baby, the reciprocity between them was low, leading to an insecure attachment. I would also suggest that there is also a link to containment here, in that the baby's emotions and arousal level were not being modulated through the process of containment, affecting both the interaction and the attachment. In order to tease out the contribution of both containment and reciprocity, this research would need to be repeated with measurements of arousal levels of both the mother and baby and observations of the presence or absence of containment.

The work of Beebe and her colleagues on the microanalysis of interactions suggests that reciprocity is one of the building blocks of attachment, in that it is possible to predict the attachment of the infant at a year old from the nature of the reciprocity in the relationship. I therefore suggest that reciprocity is the mediating mechanism through which the quality of an attachment can be changed. The work also hints at how containment is also involved in this, in that over-preoccupation with the self or over-preoccupation with the relationship both affected the quality of the attachment. This can be seen to affect the availability of the partners in the dyad to interact in the relationship, but it also affects the ability of the mother to be available for containment and for both to be involved in mutual affect regulation. I will support these suggestions by examining some of the current interventions that claim to be based on attachment theory, and I will show that the mechanisms through which they work are reciprocity and containment. This is explicit to some degree in, for instance, Robert Marvin's Circle of Security (Marvin et al., 2002).

Reciprocity, containment and attachment applied to interventions

As recently as 1999, Lieberman and Zeanah, both eminent in the field of infant mental health, suggested that 'the systematic application of attachment theory to clinical issues is still in a rudimentary stage of development' (Lieberman & Zeanah, 1999, p. 561). They gave four reasons for this. The first was that psychoanalysts are hostile to it, so that attachment theory is marginalised where psychoanalysts are involved in clinical training. The second reason was that attachment theory is not a total personality theory. It concentrates on security and protection, while clinicians work with patients with many other motivations and conflicts, so that attachment theory might seem constricting. The third reason was that its clinical applications have not been explored. Bowlby and Mary Main, although they are both clinicians, did not write about its clinical applications, but concentrated on theory and research. The fourth reason was that attachment theory emphasises behavioural observations yet is too psychoanalytic for behaviourists and too behavioural for psycho-analysts, so that it has not been embraced clinically. They review six programmes in the USA where attachment theory is used to some degree: the Infant–Parent Program at the universities of Michigan and San Francisco (Pawl & Lieberman, 1997), based on Selma Fraiberg's model (Fraiberg, 1980); the Child Trauma Research Project, San Francisco (Lieberman et al., 1997); Steps Towards Effective, Enjoyable Parenting (STEEP) in Minnesota (Erickson et al., 1992); the Rochester Program (Cicchetti & Toth, 1995); the New Orleans Program (Zeanah et al., 1997); and the Seattle Approach (Speltz, 1990). I will look at the Infant–Parent Program (IPP) in some detail, examine their inclusion of McDonough's Interaction Guidance (McDonough, 2000), describe Lieberman and Zeanah's overall con-clusion, briefly mention Mary Dozier's Infant Caregiver Project (Dozier, 2005), and then proceed to a close examination of Robert Marvin's Circle of Security (Marvin et al., 2002), which is explicitly based on attachment theory.

I am using the description of the IPP from Lieberman and Zeanah (1999). The IPP works with infants at risk. The assessment is carried out over approximately six weeks, during which time the aim is to establish a working alliance with the caregiver. The assessment and treatment sessions are unstructured, using 'questions, probings, joint play, developmental guidance, expressions of emotional support, and insight-oriented interpretations' (Lieberman & Zeanah, 1999, p. 563).

The sessions are carried out at home or in the clinic, during which 'the intervenor observes how the parents and the child relate to each other and how each of them responds to the emotions that emerge during the session' (Lieberman & Zeanah, 1999, p. 563). I suggest that the observations of how the parent relates to the child and vice versa would include the phenomenon of reciprocity, while observations of how each responds to the emotions emerging in the session would include observations of the phenomenon of containment. The aim is to help parents 'construct a more developmentally appropriate, empathic, and nuanced behavioural repertoire in their interactions with their child' (Lieberman & Zeanah, 1999, p. 563). This links both to containment, through empathy, and to reciprocity. Interestingly, Lieberman and Zeanah then view this aim as contributing to the goal of changing the quality of the attachment, that is, they, too, recognise that these are the mechanisms through which the quality of an attachment is changed. 'These interventions have the goal of helping the child become more securely reliant on the parents' (Lieberman & Zeanah, 1999, p. 563).

Lieberman and Zeanah also quote the example of Susan McDonough's Interaction Guidance (McDonough, 2000), suggesting that it shares some basic principles with attachment theory, but that it is atheoretical. However, it is based on a theory. Interaction Guidance is explicitly based on family systems theory, and McDonough describes it as a transactional model. I suggest that this programme seems to share similar principles with attachment theory because it uses the same building blocks for a changed interaction. Interaction Guidance also uses reciprocity as the mechanism through which the programme is carried out, in reviewing videotapes of the family interaction, although, again, reciprocity is not named. I suggest that it also uses the process of containment without being aware of the concept. 'As the family displays more trust in the therapeutic relationship, often members display spontaneously a wider range of emotions with the therapist . . . [O]nce the therapist judges that family members appear satisfied that their concerns were heard' (McDonough, 2000, p. 489), then the next step of the session is carried out and the play is videoed. I suggest that containment is the mechanism through which the participants are able to feel safe enough to show more emotion and then feel that they have been heard or understood.

Lieberman and Zeanah conclude that, although there are differences between the seven programmes which they reviewed, they all 'share the overarching principle that sensitive and age-appropriate responsiveness to a child's signals needs to characterize both a parent's and therapist's stance' (Lieberman & Zeanah, 1999, p. 572). I think that this conclusion would be more appropriate to a review of interventions based on reciprocity than attachment! But it is interesting that this is the conclusion of a review of interventions linked to attachment. That is, working with reciprocity is taken for granted within their review of the interventions. Indeed, the centrality of reciprocity is explicitly stated in the concluding sentence of the review that the therapist 'explicitly attempts to reestablish a working relationship characterized by the hallmarks of attachment theory – reciprocity, emotional contingency, and mutual trust' (Lieberman & Zeanah, 1999, p. 572). Emotional contingency could be linked to containment. In these writings, the presence of containment is harder to infer than reciprocity, because it is a concept that would not be explicitly used by writers in the USA. However, I have pointed out where the phenomenon could occur, and I suggest that a knowledge of the concept would enrich the application of any of the interventions.

Mary Dozier's Infant Caregiver Project at the University of Delaware is based explicitly on attachment theory and focuses on the relationship between the parent and child. Her work has consistently focused on the role of attachment in the difficulties of foster children (e.g., Dozier & Manni, 2002), and this has developed into an intervention, Attachment and Biobehavioural Catch-up. In the manual for the intervention (Dozier, 2005), the use of reciprocity is implicit in the intervention. For example, in session 9, entitled 'The Importance of Touch', parents are encouraged to follow the lead of the child in breaking off contact, that is, at the look-away part of the interactive cycle. Throughout the manual, although containment is never mentioned, it can be inferred to be present through the continual references to enabling the parent help the child with fear, anxiety and overwhelming emotions. Again, containment could be a helpful explanatory concept. Interestingly, the intervention uses Robert Marvin's idea of 'shark music' from his Circle of Security programme.

Robert Marvin's Circle of Security is a small-group intervention for six mothers and/or fathers whose children are at risk. It is therefore aimed at the same population of parents as Mellow Parenting (Puckering et al., 1994), unlike those parenting groups aimed at parents with low to moderate difficulties, such as the Solihull Approach parenting groups (Douglas, 2006). The Circle of Security group meets for one and a quarter hours per week for 20 weeks, and during that time parents review videotape of their interactions with their child. The group also focuses on some educational and therapeutic work based on the Circle of Security and shark music.

The Circle of Security is a pictorial representation of Ainsworth's ideas of a Secure Base and Haven of Safety. (It is interesting, from a cultural point of view, that Robert Marvin's publication is an American one and credits the American partner in the development of attachment theory, Mary Ainsworth, rather than Bowlby from the UK, who even called his 1988 book *A Secure Base*.) The top of the circle represents the child being able to explore whether he knows that his parent is there if needed. The right-hand side of the circle represents the child's need to have his parent monitor, structure or interact in play with him. The bottom half of the circle represents the child's need for his parent to protect,

> comfort, delight, and to organize his feelings and behaviour when they go beyond his own limits of self-organization. Consistent with Bowlby's definition, the parent's formula for a secure attachment is, 'Always be bigger, stronger, wiser and kind . . . whenever possible, follow my child's need . . . whenever necessary, take charge.'
>
> (Marvin et al., 2002, p. 110)

Shark music is a memorable way of demonstrating that one's own subjective feelings can have a significant effect on how we interpret and react to a situation. A video is shown from a camera eye viewpoint, moving and turning corners along a path through the rainforest, leading down to a beach. This is accompanied by serene music, reminding me of a relaxation method – the 'imagine a beach' type plus relaxing music. The same video clip is then repeated, but this time accompanied by the musical soundtrack to the film *Jaws*. The difference in one's feelings while watching the clips is used to discuss

> how this time [after] they experience agitation and anxiety, the parents come to understand how much their own subjective experiences can affect their feelings about their child's needs. It is as if the parents had learned from their own parents that certain needs are like shark-infested waters and must be avoided. They, in turn, 'protect' their children from what they currently perceive as dangerous needs.
>
> (Marvin et al., 2002, p. 112)

The idea of shark music is frequently used throughout the programme, 'as the caregivers increase their capacity to observe and reflect on the child's signals, and to reflect on, and stay with, their own painful feelings while meeting the child's need' (Marvin et al., 2002, p. 112). I suggest that this describes a process of reciprocity and containment, observing the child's signals and learning to contain one's own feelings, and thereby creating the space for thinking.

In the abstract to their paper, Marvin et al. describe how the Circle of Security intervention is based on attachment theory, object relations theory and 'current research on early relationships' (Marvin et al., 2002, p. 107). I think this refers to reciprocity-related concepts, as these are the concepts explicitly referred to later in the paper.

Reciprocity and reciprocity-related concepts are frequently referred to in the paper. For example,

> the idea that smooth interactions between children and their caregivers are often disrupted and need 'repair'. . . . It is this ability to repair a disruption that is the essence of a secure attachment, not the lack of disruptions. This repair requires clear cues from each other, and clear understanding of, and responsiveness to, each other's signals.
>
> (Marvin et al., 2002, p. 109)

This refers to the idea of rupture and repair within reciprocity as being part of the theoretical base for this attachment-based intervention, but even more significantly, Marvin et al. are also pointing out my contention that it is an element of reciprocity that is 'the essence of a secure attachment'; that is, reciprocity is one of the building blocks underpinning the quality of an attachment. Later in the paper, reference is made to the dance of reciprocity: 'Individual differences in patterns of attachment-caregiving interactions tend to be shared by parent and child in the form of a reciprocal dance' (Marvin et al., 2002, p. 112). Attunement is mentioned together with another reference to rupture and repair: 'The close attunement between child and caregiver is, of course, occasionally disrupted, but these disruptions are easily repaired' (Marvin et al., 2002, p. 112). Mutual affect regulation is referred to: 'In most of these disordered patterns, the partners have difficulties with individual and joint affect regulation, and have anxious, complex patterns of attunement-disruption-repair that tend not to have appropriate caregiver protection of the child as predictable outcomes' (Marvin et al., 2002, p. 114). In the five goals of the intervention, the third goal refers to the ability of the adult to follow correctly the steps in the dance of the child, that is, the goal is to 'help the parents develop their observational skills, especially as these apply to reading and responding to their children's (often subtle and misleading) cues' (Marvin et al., 2002, p. 116). The reason why the paper refers to cues as misleading is that, in these children at risk, the thousands of interactions with their parents that are neither in step nor repaired lead to the children indicating their needs in non-straightforward ways.

In this attachment-based intervention, therefore, it is clear that the method of improving the quality of the attachment is based on the concept of reciprocity. But what about containment? In the abstract, the authors mention object relations theory as one of the three theories on which they have based the Circle of Security intervention. However, in the text of the paper, this is not made explicit. I will highlight areas of the text where I think object relations theory may be implicit. As this is a non-UK paper, one would not expect containment to be specifically used as a concept, but I think it can be used as a helpful explanatory concept within this paper and can be seen as underpinning the change in the quality of attachment.

Early in the paper, the protocol is described as emphasising 'the ideas of emotion regulation; interactive synchrony; states of mind regarding attachments and intimate relationships; shared states of consciousness, affect and perspectives; and reflective functioning' (Marvin et al., 2002, p. 108). 'Emotion regulation' and 'interactive synchrony' refer to reciprocity. The remainder could be seen as linking to object relations theory, although the how and why do not seem to be mentioned anywhere in the paper. 'Shared states of . . . affect' and 'reflective functioning' could be seen to relate to containment. Later, the authors state that 'each caregiver is guided at her or his own pace toward increased skill in reading the child's cues, reflecting on the child's (inferred) thoughts and feelings, and reflecting on her or his own feelings, plans and behaviour' (Marvin et al., 2002, p. 116). The first section refers to reciprocity, but the second and third sections allude to the function of containment as being able to process or manage emotions so that reflection can take place, instead of being overwhelmed by the emotion. The fourth goal of the intervention (out of five) is 'to develop a process of reflective dialogue in the group – a skill that the parent can then use internally; this process is viewed as the central dynamic for change' (Marvin et al., 2002, p. 116). This internal capacity for reflection, again, could be seen as relating to the successful outcome of containment. The fifth goal, 'supporting the parents' empathic shift from defensive process to empathy for their children' (Marvin et al., 2002, p. 116), could also be seen as relating to containment, although empathy is not the same phenomenon. Having a sense of someone else's emotions is only part of the process of containment. The description of the lower half of the Circle of Security states that the child's need is for his parent to protect, 'comfort, delight, and to organize his feelings and behaviour when they go beyond his own limits of self-organization'. This relates more to containment than mutual affect regulation. In mutual affect regulation, both the child and the parent are involved, but in containment the parent has the major role, as in this description. Therefore, the theory is then that as the child's emotions and anxiety are contained he builds up the internal capacity to manage himself.

In the paper, Marvin et al. describe the interaction of a mother, Candy, with her daughter, Paula. Candy's mother was 16 years old when Candy was born and treated her daughter more as a sister, abdicating much of her parental responsibility, with the result that Candy took charge. Candy is now repeating this pattern with her own daughter, Paula. By seeing their interaction on the videotape and realising that she was repeating this pattern, Candy became able to change her behaviour and access her own ability to parent. The following vignette, I think, illustrates Candy's new-found ability to contain her daughter's emotions at the seven-week follow-up, although this is inferred from the description and the result.

> During the second reunion, Paula makes it clear that she is upset and angry at her mother for having gone, and continues to show signs of distress for several minutes after Candy's return. Candy seeks to provide comfort, haltingly offering Kleenex, toys and physical comfort. But Paula's upset continues until her mother firmly places Paula on her lap, comforts her physically, and gets her involved with a toy. Only then does Paula calm, and come to rest in her mother's presence.
>
> (Marvin et al., 2002, p. 121)

There is an indication of Candy's shift in attitude, from hesitantly interacting with her upset daughter and attempting to mop up the tears to being much more present in the interaction and perhaps more emotionally available to her daughter. I infer from the end result, i.e. that Paula calms down, that her mother has been able to help Paula with her upset. It would require a much fuller description of the videotape than 'comforts her physically' to describe the process of containment. One can only hypothesise that Candy managed to convey her understanding of her daughter's feelings, that this time she was not overwhelmed by them and was able to help her daughter process them. Containment provides the concept to describe this, and, together with mutual affect regulation, provides the mechanism for emotion regulation that is at the heart of this intervention.

I propose that the concept of containment is perhaps required more than mutual affect regulation (although mutual affect regulation will also be helpful as a concept, as is mentioned in the paper: 'the partners have difficulties with individual and joint affect regulation' (Marvin et al., 2002, p. 114)) with this particular population of parents and children, because of the strength of feeling on both sides and because of the requirement for the adults usually to increase their presence as parents and take on more responsibility within the interactions. As outlined earlier, mutual affect regulation involves both partners in the interaction and refers to changing negative emotions to positive ones. It also refers to a lower intensity of emotion. For instance, Sue Reid's interaction with Georgie (Reid, 1990), described previously, with the strength of his terror, requires containment, not mutual affect regulation.

The Circle of Security intervention explicitly uses the concept of reciprocity and reciprocity-related concepts. Marvin et al. also state that being able to repair the disruptions in reciprocal interactions is the basis for a secure attachment. Although the authors state that object relations theory is one of the three theories used in the intervention, it is not explicit in the text. It is possible, however, to link elements of the intervention to containment. Empathy is one element of containment, and this is a specific goal of the Circle of Security intervention. I suggest that this supports my hypothesis that both reciprocity and containment are the building blocks for the quality of an attachment, as both of these are used to change the quality of the attachments within this attachment-based intervention.

All the programmes described above concentrate on the relationship. The nuts and bolts of the architectural scaffolding of a relationship include reciprocity and containment. Attachment, as a biological mechanism, is also part of the scaffolding, but the mechanism to build the quality of the attachment includes containment and reciprocity.

Additional evidence from neurobiology

Some of the evidence for the organic substrate of containment and reciprocity has been described earlier. The evidence for the organic basis of the quality of an attachment supports my contention that reciprocity and containment are the building blocks for it. For instance, Schore (2003) summarised the organic substrate of reciprocity, which in turn underpins attachment, as follows: 'The right hemisphere contributes to the development of reciprocal interactions within the mother–infant regulatory system and mediates the capacity for biological synchronicity, the regulatory mechanism of attachment' (Schore, 2003, p. 23).

In his 2001 paper, Schore describes in detail the neurobiology of a secure attachment. He contends that attachment theory is in essence a regulatory theory and that the mechanism through which the baby's brain develops is through the millisecond-to-millisecond reciprocal interaction. As the synchrony is established, the baby's arousal level is regulated. Both containment and reciprocity are involved. For containment 'to act as a regulator of the infant's arousal, she must be able to regulate her own arousal state' (Schore, 2001, p. 20). For the adult to help the infant to regulate himself, the adult has to be able 'to monitor and regulate her own affect, especially negative affect. The regulation of her own affective state, as well as the child's may be an emotionally demanding task' (Schore, 2001, p. 20). This regulation underpins attachment: 'These arousal-regulating transactions, which continue throughout the first year, underlie the formation of an attachment bond between the infant and the primary caregiver' (Schore, 2001, p. 20). Schore describes the effects of a reciprocal interaction, as, for example, increasing 'N-methyl-D-aspartate (NMDA) receptor levels, resulting in elevated BDNF and synaptogenesis in the infant's brain' (Schore, 2001, p. 25). He also links Bowlby with Brazelton:

> The critical period of anterior cingulate-driven limbic maturation thus overlaps Bowlby's (1969) phase of 'attachment-in-the-making'. . . . Brazelton (2000) describes the emergence in the second quarter of the first year of a second homeostatic control system, one associated with a mutual reciprocal feedback system; although an advance of the former control system, it is still 'an immature psychophysiological system'. I suggest that this system can be identified as a maturing anterior cingulate which now hierarchically controls the earlier amygdala-dominated limbic configuration.
>
> (Schore, 2001, p. 34)

Schore is not an easy read! However, he has brought together the evidence of actual brain development in the context of a reciprocal, containing relationship which affects the quality of the attachment, and this, in turn, affects the development of the brain. This, therefore, can set up either a vicious or a virtuous cycle, in which brain development is enhanced or in which it is not facilitated. He has summarised the research across disciplines about how development is supported by a positive attachment and how, conversely, development is adversely affected by a lack of attachment (Schore, 2001).

Attachment, bonding and reciprocity

As a footnote to this chapter, I would like, very briefly, to link attachment, bonding and reciprocity. Parents often describe how they have or have not 'bonded' with their infant. It seems to me that bonding is part of the attachment system, when the caregiver and infant look into each other's eyes, and the adult has an intense sensation, somewhat akin to falling in love, an intense feeling of connectedness to this other being. Bonding is perhaps mediated through reciprocity and is also linked to the sudden intense feeling in the previous descriptions of the work of child psychotherapists with children.

Although it was not possible to identify material within the vignettes quoted earlier in this book to demonstrate the relationship between containment, reciprocity and attachment, further evidence has been cited that indicates that containment and reciprocity are the mechanisms underpinning the quality of an attachment. By understanding containment and reciprocity, we can utilise the concepts in the work with a relationship in order that the attachment system may be changed.

11 Integrating containment and reciprocity in work with children

Development occurs within a context, and the most important context for children is the relationship. Tronick and Weinberg stated that the infant's

> understanding of the world of objects, no matter how primitive, is dependent on establishing inter-subjective states with others and the mutual construction of meaning. Thus the establishment of social processes is the primary process of development and the understanding of the inanimate world is secondary to it.
>
> (Tronick & Weinberg, 1997, p. 55)

Examples from research in both the psychotherapy world and the world of child development have been quoted to show that both containment and reciprocity are central to relationships. Containment, reciprocity and attachment all have in common the emphasis on the importance of early relationships.

Theory informs practice and practice informs theory. I have put forward a number of ideas in this book, so I would like to take this opportunity, as the end of the book is in sight, of summarising the theoretical developments and outlining some ideas of how the theory can inform practical developments.

Theoretical developments

A contemporary definition of containment, together with a definition of reciprocity, has emerged from an examination of literature from different sources, from the psychoanalytic world and from the child development world. This close look at the literature has enabled me to clarify the relationship between reciprocity and the reciprocity-type concepts of attunement, intersubjectivity and mutual affect regulation. I have also been able to use other research material to show that containment and reciprocity are the building blocks underpinning the quality of an attachment. From the data, in conjunction with a review of other research, I have outlined several characteristics of containment and reciprocity and argued that they exist on separate but related continuums.

The continuum for containment can be visualised as being defined by the strength of projection. At one end is macrocontainment, which emphasises the idea of parts of the self or personality being projected and contained; containment, in the middle of the continuum, emphasises the idea of strong emotions being projected and contained. At the other end of the continuum is microcontainment, where less intense emotions are passed to and fro between two people or the baby and mother, and where the baby also has a rudimentary ability to contain emotions.

The reciprocity continuum can be visualised as being defined by the degree to which it is mediated through the unconscious mind. At one end is amplified reciprocity, which is deliberate and used for bringing the relationship to the attention of the other person, where the other is currently unavailable for contact through the usual reciprocity. This unavailability might be through nature or nurture or a combination of the two. In the middle of the reciprocity continuum is reciprocity, where both persons participate in the dance and rhythm of the interaction, which can sometimes include an intense feeling of closeness to the other person. At the other end of the continuum is mutual affect regulation where the emphasis is on both persons being involved in regulating emotion.

The continuums link at microcontainment. In both microcontainment and mutual affect regulation, I have argued that the mother and the baby are active participants, with the baby having a rudimentary ability to contain from birth, which enables him to participate with the mother in regulating the affect of the mother as well as the mother participating with the baby to regulate the affect of the baby.

The conscious and the unconscious mind are both involved in containment and in reciprocity. Containment is largely mediated through the unconscious, but it can be facilitated through the conscious mind. Reciprocity can be deliberately mediated consciously, but it, too, usually occurs at the level of the unconscious.

Since there is wide variation in the capabilities of infants, they generally have some capacity present from birth to participate in reciprocal interactions. They also have some capacity for containment present from birth at the microcontainment end of the containment continuum.

Sometimes containment precedes reciprocity and sometimes reciprocity precedes containment. In different situations, one may facilitate the other and vice versa. In many of the situations quoted from the literature, it was possible to show that both were present in particular interactions. It was not possible to detail in which situations one might precede the other.

Attachment itself is a biological mechanism, but the building blocks for the quality of an attachment are containment and reciprocity.

The concepts applied to working with children

Many current programmes and theories might find a consideration of containment and reciprocity to be helpful, both as explanatory concepts and as indicators for therapeutic interventions. I have already indicated above where I think the concepts might be helpful when one is looking at theories. Here I am going to concentrate on how they can be helpful in practical applications, for mental health specialists already using containment, for specialists already using reciprocity, and for mental health specialists not using either. These concepts can also be extremely helpful for those who work with children but who are not mental health specialists.

Psychoanalytic psychotherapists are well versed in using the concept of containment in their work. I think a consideration of the concept of reciprocity would also be helpful, for two reasons. The first is for the development of theory, as discussed above, and the second is to contribute to technique by informing thought and action in the present moment in the therapy room, and by illuminating the session when reflecting upon it in retrospect.

From the evidence reviewed earlier, from the excerpts of therapeutic interactions, it can be seen that issues concerned with reciprocity are present in our consulting rooms already. They may be especially vivid with young children and those who have early primary disappointments, that is, most of our caseload. However, at present, only a tiny proportion of these interactions reaches our full awareness. This is likely to be because psychoanalytic psychotherapy does not have a name for this interaction. The name exists, as reciprocity, but within another discipline, that of child development research. I have already shown that psychotherapists working with children under five years of age have begun to consider reciprocity within their work, and reciprocity is used with children on the autism spectrum. The work of Alvarez, using amplified reciprocity with children on the autism spectrum (Alvarez, 1992), has been described earlier; here the therapist exaggerates the steps in the dance in order to connect with the child in what Alvarez has called 'reclamation'. However, generally, the process of reciprocity is not named and therefore is not recognised within psychoanalytic work.

I think that three points of technique arise in relation to reciprocity. The first is to allow experiences to happen and to wait; the second is to be aware of the implications of 'chase and dodge' and 'rupture and repair'; and the third is to be able to use the process of reciprocity within sessions.

A knowledge of reciprocity might inform the timing of interpretations or interaction. One implication of knowing about the steps of the dance would be not to interpret anything immediately, within the look-away cycle of reciprocity. That is not to say that interpretations should never be given immediately, but only that, where the therapist and child are operating within that dance of reciprocity, the steps of the dance, especially the presence of a look-away cycle, need to be taken into account. Brazelton's study showed that the baby needs time to rest, to assimilate experiences, and any attempt by the mother to interact at this time breaks the flow between them. The pause required may be related to Schore's (1996) and Perry's (1995) neurobiological discoveries of the neural connections being laid down in the baby's brain as a direct result of the experience he has just had. Timing of interpretations is often thought about in the literature (cf. Bott Spillius, 1988). The timing of interpretations, speech or intervention of any kind on the part of the therapist can be helped by careful consideration of the pattern of interaction described by Brazelton et al. (1974) between the baby and the mother.

> When the mother can allow for the cyclic turning away from her, which seems to be necessary for the infant, she can be assured of longer periods of attention when he turns back to her. One of our mothers was particularly striking in her capacity to subside as he decreased his attention to her. She relaxed back in her chair smiling softly, reducing other activity such as vocalising and moving, waiting for him to return. When he did look back, she began slowly to add behaviour on behaviour, as if she were feeling out how much he could master . . . she provided an atmosphere that led to longer periods of interaction.
>
> (Brazelton et al., 1974, p. 66)

Attending to the pattern of interaction and knowing about not intervening within the look-away cycle may facilitate the interaction.

The second point of technique is to be aware of the elements of 'rupture and repair' and 'chase and dodge'. Therapists, as people, will usually have an intuitive recognition of the ruptures within the interaction, ruptures caused by themselves as well as the child, so that they can then facilitate the repair. A conscious knowledge may help recognition of when the therapist ruptures the interaction and thus facilitate thinking about the counter-transference. Similarly, it may also help recognition of rupture caused by the child within the minutiae of the interaction, and this may facilitate thinking about the transference. It may also help recognition of repair, by both the therapist and the child, at a macro-level and a micro-level and therefore enable an understanding of both the therapist's and child's contributions to the relationship. One of the skills of psychotherapists is putting feelings and actions into words. There may be times when, as well as informing action, an understanding of reciprocity will enable the therapist to put the pattern of their dance into words. If psychotherapists video their work, allowing detailed examination of the session, then a knowledge of reciprocity will also help to illuminate the interaction.

The therapist can also be aware of 'chase and dodge'. With some children in some situations, it may be appropriate to 'chase' them; for example, by using amplified reciprocity with children on the autistic spectrum. This would require a conscious knowledge of 'chase and dodge' and the look-away cycle in order to inform the intensity and timing of the interaction that will bring the child into an interaction, rather than forcing them to dodge it. This, as discussed previously, can be linked to Meltzer's idea of temperature and distance of affect within sessions. For instance, sometimes the therapist will need to downregulate the emotional level in the session if it becomes apparent that the patient is 'dodging' the therapist. Chasing the patient in this situation would be counterproductive, as it would lead to more extreme dodging by the patient, just as the babies in Brazelton's study had a range of options open to them, from averting their eyes to turning their heads away.

The third point of technique is that knowledge of the cycle of reciprocity can be used to reach children in the sessions. Some children who already have a responsive internal object can respond immediately to interpretations. Other children may need their preconception of a responsive object to meet a realisation in order to produce the concept: 'the mating of pre-conception with sense impressions to produce a conception' (Bion, 1962a, p. 91). The therapist, as shown in the clinical examples quoted, may need to engage in reciprocity with the child, linking this to interpretations or progressing onto interpretations. Many of the vignettes I have quoted from child psychotherapists show that the therapists have 'naturally' engaged with children who needed this type of interaction before the children could move on.

I have outlined above how a consideration of reciprocity might be helpful to mental health specialists who already explicitly use containment in their work, such as psychoanalytic psychotherapists. Containment might also be helpful to mental health specialists who explicitly use reciprocity in their research or in their therapeutic work. To consider the latter, I hope I have already indicated how containment could be helpful when examining the interactions between mothers and their infants in research, in Beebe's work or Tronick's, for example. In therapeutic work, the concept could perhaps be helpful to anyone who is using an integrative approach to their work; people who, by definition, are open to looking at how different theories can contribute to an explanation of why something works and to the design and redesign of different approaches. For instance, the concept of containment could be helpful in therapeutic programmes such as Susan McDonough's Interaction Guidance, Robert Marvin's Circle of Security, or, indeed, Berry Brazelton's Touchpoints.

Both concepts, containment and reciprocity, can be helpful for those who work with children but are not mental health specialists, such as health visitors (in the UK), children's centre workers, family workers, children's nurses, social workers, teachers and education professionals, and Early Head Start workers (in the USA). One study examined the effect on health visitors of a two-day training on the Solihull Approach (Douglas & Ginty, 2001). The Solihull Approach is an integrated model, in which containment and reciprocity are two of the elements, together with behaviour management as the third element (e.g., Douglas, 2004a). The main findings of the study were that the short training had an impact on 88 per cent of the health visitors. It improved consistency of practice and increased the amount of time taken for assessment, without affecting the overall time of an intervention, because intervention time was decreased. It increased health visitors' job satisfaction and often increased their confidence in their own skills.

Knowing about containment can be helpful in many ways, some of which have already been described. It can prepare workers to be available to emotional communication, to be open to listen to the other person. This apparently simple thought can transform the work and the effectiveness of workers who have previously been orientated towards giving advice. This stance can be helpful for many professional groups, such as general practitioners and paediatricians, even if they do not have the time in their practice to co-construct the whole story. To take the health visitor as an example, a knowledge of containment can result in the practical step of making sure that time is scheduled into the diary to listen, and this also results in better assessment. It prepares the health visitor for the impact of another's emotions, rather than avoiding this, with the consequent benefits also then being lost. It can make both the worker and the organisation aware of the support needed for the worker to function effectively. Containment, together with reciprocity and attachment, provide the theoretical rationale of why it is important to give people notice of planned absences or of leaving the job – a seemingly simple consideration and yet apparently often neglected, this was a major concern that emerged from a qualitative study of mothers' views of health visitors (Maunders et al., in press). Even with a small number of contacts with the health visitor, mothers were very concerned to know about absence. Naming containment can thus prepare the worker for the emotional aspect of work, the consequences of which should not be underestimated.

A qualitative study (Whitehead & Douglas, 2005) used in-depth interviewing of health visitors to tease out further qualitative information about why the Solihull Approach was helpful for health visitors and the impact it had upon their practice. There were some interesting findings. They had developed an increased understanding of the importance of assessment in 'focusing more on emotions and trying to understand the story rather than rushing in and trying to solve the problem' (Whitehead & Douglas, 2005, p. 21). They 'developed a better understanding of how problems developed and also why previous approaches may not have worked' (Whitehead & Douglas, 2005, p. 21). It was helpful to have a structure to work within. There was a feeling of being able to identify problems earlier so that fewer older children needed to be seen. The model enabled health visitors to change the way in which they were engaging with families, empowering parents to find their own answers. 'One health visitor described how it increased the confidence of the families as well as that of the professional and also helped parents to understand their children better, contain their anxieties and adapt their parenting accordingly' (Whitehead & Douglas, 2005, p. 21). Part of the reason why using the

Solihull Approach increased job satisfaction was attributed to the stimulation of lifelong learning. One health visitor reported:

> The other thing about the Solihull Approach is that you get this initial sudden change and you think 'wow', but then there is this on-going learning curve, so it's not like you get this sudden shift and then you're an expert. You get this sudden burst that's astounding but then you still have to keep learning and every now and then you get these little peaks of learning.
>
> (Whitehead & Douglas, 2005, p. 22)

I think that the concepts of containment and reciprocity contribute to lifelong learning because of their profound nature. Their simplicity allows those with experience of working with families to grasp quickly the initial implications of the concepts in a short introductory training of two days. But because there is a depth to each concept there is always more to learn.

An initial small-scale study also showed that health visitors using the Solihull Approach were effective (Douglas & Brennan, 2004), reducing symptoms, parents' anxiety about the difficulty, and parents' own general anxiety levels. This result has been repeated with a larger sample with a control group in another area of the UK (Milford et al., 2006). Detailed descriptions and supporting material for applying these concepts to clinical work can be found in *The Solihull Approach: The First Five Years Resource Pack* (Douglas, 2004a) and *The Solihull Approach: The School Years Resource Pack* (Douglas, 2004b).

Sometimes group interventions are shaped by what works practically and then the theory is developed to explain why they work. This is one way to innovate. However, it can be more effective to take those conceptual building blocks that work and then design a group intervention, tweaking the practical application in pilot sessions. Robert Marvin's Circle of Security is an example of how knowledge of reciprocity and reciprocity-related theories have informed the design of the intervention, although I think that a knowledge of containment would be helpful to explain why it is effective. The Solihull Approach Parenting Group (Douglas, 2006) is another example. The model of the Solihull Approach (containment, reciprocity and behaviour management) had already been developed for work with individual families and was being applied to group work, including antenatal groups, postnatal groups and breastfeeding groups. It had also been integrated into parenting groups by Sue Brough and Mary Rheeston at Solihull's Sure Start project. A project group was formed to develop this work, weaving the theoretical concepts more explicitly through a two-hour-per-week, ten-week group, manualising each week of the course so that others could run it, and adapting it to the needs of each individual group. The manualised course was piloted and evaluated, with adaptations made to the manual arising from the experience of the groups. A one-day facilitators' training was also developed, again making the concepts of containment and reciprocity explicit. Research is again being carried out to determine the impact upon the practitioners of facilitating parenting groups when the concepts of containment and reciprocity are made explicit throughout the material.

To conclude, it has been interesting to use Hegel's idea of the dialectic to synthesise the psychoanalytic concept of containment with the child development concept of reciprocity. My examination of child development research material and psychoanalytic psychotherapeutic examples has indicated that containment and reciprocity are both part of wider continuums; they are linked and they are the building blocks of the quality of an attachment. I have outlined some theoretical implications, together with implications for technique.

I have found containment and reciprocity to be useful in my own work. I hope that this book will help to make them available to a wider audience where professional boundaries and continental drift have isolated them one from another.

References

Ainsworth, M., Blehar, M., Waters, E. and Wall, S. (1978). *Patterns of attachment: A psychological study of the strange situation.* Hillsdale, NJ: Lawrence Erlbaum Associates.

Altman, N., Briggs, R., Frankel, J., Gensler, D. and Pantone, P. (2002). *Relational child psychotherapy.* New York: Other Press.

Alvarez, A. (1992). *Live company.* London: Routledge.

Alvarez, A. (1999). Addressing the deficit: Developmentally informed psychotherapy with passive, 'undrawn' children. In A. Alvarez and S. Reid (eds), *Autism and personality.* New York: Routledge.

Anderson, R. (1998). Suicidal behaviour and its meaning in adolescence. In R. Anderson and A. Dartington (eds), *Facing it out.* London: Duckworth.

Astor, J. (1995). *Michael Fordham: Innovations in analytical psychology.* London: Routledge.

Atkinson, R., Brace Atkinson, R., Smith, E. and Bem, D. (1993). *Introduction to psychology.* Orlando, FL: Harcourt College Publishers.

Ayres, A. J. (1979). *Sensory integration and the child.* Los Angeles, CA: Western Psychological Services.

Bakermans-Kranenburg, M., Juffer, F. and van Ijzendoorn, M. (1998). Interventions with video feedback and attachment discussions. *Infant Mental Health Journal, 19,* 202–219.

Balbernie, R. (2003) *Early intervention and infant mental health: Relationship based services for high-risk families.* London: Child Psychotherapy Trust.

Bartram, P. (1999). Sean: From solitary invulnerability to the beginnings of reciprocity at very early infantile levels. In A. Alvarez and S. Reid (eds), *Autism and personality.* New York: Routledge.

Bateson, M. C. (1971). *Quarterly progress report.* Research Laboratory of Electronics, Massachusetts Institute of Technology. Cambridge, MA: MIT Press.

Beebe, B. (2003). Brief mother–infant treatment: Psychoanalytically informed video feedback. *Infant Mental Health Journal, 24,* 24–52.

Beebe, B. and Lachmann, F. (1988). The contribution of mother–infant mutual influence to the origins of self and object representations. *Psychoanalytic Psychology*, 5, 304–337.

Beebe, B. and Lachmann, F. (1998). Co-constructing inner and relational processes. *Psychoanalytic Psychology*, 15, 480–516.

Beebe, B. and Lachmann, F. (2002). *Infant research and adult treatment*. Hillsdale, NJ: Analytic Press.

Beebe, B. and Stern, D. (1977). Engagement–disengagement and early object experiences. In N. Freedman and S. Grand (eds), *Communicative structures and psychic structures*. New York: Plenum.

Beebe, B., Lachmann, F. and Jaffe, J. (1997). Mother–infant interaction structures and presymbolic self and object representations. *Psychoanalytic Dialogues*, 7, 133–182.

Beebe, B., Jaffe J., Lachmann, F., Feldstein, S., Crown, C. and Jasnow, J. (2000). Systems models in development and psychoanalysis: The case of vocal rhythm coordination and attachment. *Infant Mental Health Journal*, 21, 99–122.

Benoit, D. and Parker, K. (1994). Stability and transmission of attachment across three generations. *Child Development*, 65, 1444–1456.

Besnard, S., Courtois, M., Fayolle, A., Miller, L. and Rustin, M. (1998). Three observations of young infants, with commentary on initial patterns of communication and containment between the babies and their parents. *International Journal of Infant Observation, 1*, 51–70.

Bick, E. (1964). Notes on infant observation in psychoanalytic training. *International Journal of Psycho-Analysis*, 45, 558–566.

Bick, E. (1968). The experience of the skin in early object relations. *International Journal of Psychoanalysis*, 49, 484–486.

Bion, W. R. (1959/1993). Attacks on linking. In *Second thoughts*. London: Karnac.

Bion, W. R. (1962a/1991). *Learning from experience*. London: Karnac.

Bion, W. R. (1962b/1993). A theory of thinking. In *Second thoughts*. London: Karnac.

Bion, W. R. (1970). *Attention and interpretation*. London: Karnac.

Bion, W. R. (1990). *Brazilian lectures*. London: Karnac.

Boston, M. (1991). The splitting image: The research perspective. In R. Szur and S. Miller (eds), *Extending horizons. Psychoanalytic psychotherapy with children, adolescents and families*. London: Karnac.

Bott Spillius, E. (1988). *Melanie Klein today*. Vol. 2. *Mainly practice*. London: Routledge.

Bower, T. (1982). *Development in infancy*. San Francisco, CA: W. H. Freeman.

Bowlby, J. (1951). *Maternal care and mental health*. WHO Monograph Series, No. 2. Geneva: World Health Organization.

Bowlby, J. (1969). *Attachment and loss*. Vol. 1. *Attachment*. London: Hogarth Press and the Institute of Psychoanalysis.

Bowlby, J. (1973). *Attachment and loss.* Vol. 2. *Separation: Anxiety and anger.* London: Hogarth Press and the Institute of Psychoanalysis.

Bowlby, J. (1988). *A secure base.* London: Routledge.

Braten, S. (1987). Dialogic mind: The infant and the adult in proto conversation. In M. Carvallo (ed.), *Nature, cognition and systems.* Dordrecht: D. Reidel.

Brazelton, T. B. (1980). New knowledge about the infant from current research: Implications for psychoanalysis. Paper presented at the American Psychoanalytic Association, San Francisco, California.

Brazelton, T. B. (2000). In response to Louis Sander's challenging paper. *Infant Mental Health Journal, 21,* 52–62.

Brazelton, T. B., Koslowski, B. and Main, M. (1974). The origins of reciprocity: The early mother–infant interaction. In M. Lewis and L. Rosenblum (eds), *The effect of the infant on its caregiver.* London: Wiley.

Breakwell, G., Hammond, S. and Fife-Shaw, C. (1995). *Research methods in psychology.* London: Sage Publications.

Britton, R. (1989). The missing link. In R. Britton, M. Feldman and E. O'Shaughnessy (eds), *The Oedipus complex today.* London: Karnac Books.

Campbell, S. (2004). *Watch me grow.* London: St Martin's Press.

Cassidy, J. and Shaver, P. (1999). *Handbook of attachment.* New York: Guilford Press.

Chapple, E. (1970). *Culture and biological man.* New York: Holt, Rinehart and Winston.

Cicchetti, D. and Toth, S. (1995). Child maltreatment and attachment organization: Implications for intervention. In S. Goldberg, R. Muir and J. Kerr (eds), *Attachment theory: Social, developmental and clinical perspectives.* Hillsdale, NJ: Analytic Press.

Clifton, R. (2001). Lessons from infants: 1960–2000. *Infancy, 2,* 285–309.

Cohen, N. J., Muir, E., Parker, C. J., Brown, M., Lojkasek, M., Muir, R. and Barwick, M. (1999). Watch, wait and wonder: Testing the effectiveness of a new approach to mother–infant psychotherapy. *Infant Mental Health Journal, 20,* 429–451.

Cramer, B. (1987). Objective and subjective aspects of parent–infant relations: An attempt at correlation between infant studies and clinical work. In J. Osofsky (ed.), *Handbook of infant development.* New York: Wiley.

Cramer, B. (1998). Mother–infant psychotherapies: A widening scope in technique. *Infant Mental Health Journal, 19,* 151–167.

Crockenburg, S. and Leerkes, E. (2000). Infant social and emotional development in family context. In C. Zeanah (ed.), *Handbook of infant mental health* (2nd edn). New York: Guilford Press.

Crockenburg, S., Lyons-Ruth, K. and Dickstein, S. (1993). The family context of infant mental health. In C. Zeanah (ed.), *Handbook of infant mental health.* New York: Guilford Press.

Daws, D. (1991). Infants' sleep problems. In R. Szur and S. Miller (eds), *Extending horizons.* London: Karnac.

Daws, D. (1993). *Through the night: Helping parents and sleepless infants.* London: Free Association Books.

DeCasper, A. and Carstens, A. (1981). Contingencies of stimulation: Effects on learning and emotion in neonates. *Infant Behaviour and Development, 4,* 19–35.

Denzin, N. and Lincoln, Y. (eds), *Handbook of qualitative research.* Thousand Oaks, CA: Sage.

De Wolff, M. and van Ijzendoorn, M. (1997). Sensitivity and attachment: A meta-analysis on parental antecedents of infant attachment. *Child Development, 68,* 571–591.

Department for Education and Skills (2001). Questions about mental health. *Promoting children's mental health within early years and school settings.* London: Department for Education and Skills.

Doherty-Sneddon, G. (2004). Don't look now . . . I'm trying to think. *The Psychologist, 17,* 82–85.

Douglas, H. (2002). Containment and reciprocity. *International Journal of Infant Observation, 4,* 29–47.

Douglas, H. (2004a). *The Solihull Approach resource pack: The first five years* (4th edn). Cambridge: Jill Rogers Associates.

Douglas, H. (2004b). *The Solihull Approach resource pack: The school years.* Cambridge: Jill Rogers Associates.

Douglas, H. (2006). *The Solihull Approach parenting group: Supporting parent/child relationships. Facilitator's resource pack.* Cambridge: Jill Rogers Associates.

Douglas, H. and Brennan, A. (2004). Containment, reciprocity and behaviour management: Preliminary evaluation of a brief early intervention (the Solihull Approach) for families with infants and young children. *International Journal of Infant Observation, 7,* 89–107.

Douglas, H. and Ginty, M. (2001). The Solihull Approach: Changes in health visitor practice. *Community Practitioner, 74,* 222–224.

Dozier, M. (2005). *Attachment and biobehavioural catch-up: An intervention targeting the relationship between parent and child.* Manual of Infant Caregiver Project. Newark, DE: University of Delaware.

Dozier, M. and Manni, M. (2002). Recognizing the special needs of infants' and toddlers' foster parents: Development of a relational intervention. *Zero to Three Bulletin, 22,* 7–13.

Dubinsky, A. (1997). Theoretical overview. In M. Rustin, M. Rhode, A. Dubinsky and H. Dubinsky (eds), *Psychotic states in children.* London: Duckworth.

Emanuel, L. (1997). Facing the damage together. *Journal of Child Psychotherapy, 23,* 279–302.

Emanuel, R. (1984). Primary disappointment. *Journal of Child Psychotherapy, 10,* 71–87.

Ekman, P. (1983). Autonomic nervous activity distinguishes among emotions. *Science, 221,* 1208–1210.

Erickson, M., Korfmacher, J. and Egeland, B. (1992). Attachments past and present: Implications for the therapeutic intervention with mother–infant dyads. *Development and Psychopathology*, *4*, 495–507.

Fantz, R. and Nevis, S. (1967). Perceptual preferences and perceptual-cognitive development in early infancy. *Merrill-Palmer Quarterly*, *13*, 77–108.

Fernald, A. (1992). Human maternal vocalizations to infants as biologically relevant signals: An evolutionary perspective. In J. Barkow, L. Cosmides and J. Tooby (eds), *The adapted mind; evolutionary psychology and the generation of culture*. Oxford: Oxford University Press.

Fonagy, P. (2001). *Attachment theory and psychoanalysis*. New York: Other Press.

Fonagy, P., Steele, H. and Steele, M. (1991). Maternal representations of attachment during pregnancy predict the organisation of infant–mother attachment at one year of age. *Child Development*, *62*, 891–905.

Fraiberg, S. (1980). *Clinical studies in infant mental health: The first year of life*. New York: Basic Books.

Freud, S. (1915/1991). Instincts and their vicissitudes. In *Freud: On metapsychology*. London: Penguin.

Freud, S. (1917/1991). A metapsychological supplement to the theory of dreams. In *Freud: On metapsychology*. London: Penguin.

Freud, S. (1920/1991). Beyond the pleasure principle. In *Freud: On metapsychology*. London: Penguin.

Freud, S. (1940/1991). Splitting of the ego in the process of defence. In *Freud: On metapsychology*. London: Penguin.

Garland, C. (1998). Issues in treatment; a case of rape. In C. Garland (ed.), *Understanding trauma; a psychoanalytical approach*. London: Duckworth.

Gergely, G. (1991). Developmental reconstructions: Infancy from the point of view of psychoanalysis and developmental psychology. *Psychoanalysis and Contemporary Thought*, *14*, 3–55.

Ghent, E. (1992). Foreword. In N. J. Skolnick and S. C. Warshaw (eds), *Relational perspectives in psychoanalysis*. Hillsdale, NJ: Analytic Press.

Gianino, A. and Tronick, E. Z. (1988). The mutual regulation model: The infant's self and interactive regulation coping and defense. In T. Field, P. McCabe and N. Schneiderman (eds), *Stress and Coping*. Hillsdale, NJ: Lawrence Erlbaum Associates, Inc.

Glaser, D. (2005). Interview with *NovaScienceNow*. www.pbs.org/wgbh/nova/sciencenow/3204 (accessed 1 August 2005).

Gottman, J. (1981). *Time-series analysis*. Cambridge: Cambridge University Press.

Gould, D. and Tuffey, S. (1996). Zones of optimal functioning research: A review and critique. *Anxiety, Stress and Coping*, *9*, 53–68.

Greenspan, S. (1981). *Psychopathology and adaptation in infancy and early childhood: Principles of early diagnosis and preventive intervention*. New York: International University Press.

Greenspan, S. and Wieder, S. (1993). Regulatory disorders. In C. Zeanah (ed.), *Handbook of infant mental health*. New York: Guilford Press.

Hanin, Y. (1980). A study of anxiety in sports. In W. F. Straub (ed.), *Sport psychology: An analysis of athlete behaviour*. Ithaca, NY: Mouvement.

Hebb, D. O. (1949). *The organization of behavior*. New York: Wiley.

Heimann, P. (1950). On counter-transference. *International Journal of Psychoanalysis*, *31*, 81–84.

Hepper, P. (2005). Unravelling our beginnings. *The Psychologist*, *18*, 474–477.

Hinshelwood, R. D. (1991). *A dictionary of Kleinian thought*. London: Free Association Books.

Hofacker, N. and Papousek, M. (1998). Disorders of excessive crying, feeding and sleeping. The Munich interdisciplinary research and intervention programme. *Infant Mental Health Journal*, *19*, 180–201.

Howes, C. (1999). Attachment relationships in the context of multiple caregivers. In J. Cassidy and P. Shaver (eds), *Handbook of attachment*. New York: Guilford Press.

Hoxter, S. (1977). Play and communication. In D. Daws and M. Boston (eds), *The child psychotherapist*. London: Karnac.

Jackson, J. (1999). It's time to stop: The examination of some technical problems in working with a violent child. Paper given at ACP 50th Birthday Conference, London.

Jaffe, J., Beebe, B., Feldstein, S., Crown, C. and Jasnow, M. (2001). Rhythms of dialogue in early infancy. *Monographs of the Society for Research in Child Development*, *66*(2), Serial No. 264, 1–132.

Jasinski, J. (2004). Pregnancy and domestic violence. *Trauma, Violence and Abuse*, *5*, 47–64.

Jones, S. and Hong, H. (2001). Onset of voluntary communication: Smiling looks to mother. *Infancy*, *2*, 353–370.

Joseph, B. (1975/1988). The patient who is difficult to reach. In E. Bott Spillius (ed.), *Melanie Klein today*. Vol. 2. *Mainly practice*. London: Routledge.

Joseph B. (1985/1988). Transference: The total situation. In E. Bott Spillius (ed.), *Melanie Klein today*. Vol. 2. *Mainly practice*. London: Routledge.

Karr-Morse, R. and Wiley, M. (1997). *Ghosts from the nursery*. New York: Atlantic Monthly Press.

Keysers, C., Kohler, E., Umilta, M., Nanetti, L., Fogassi, L. and Gellese, V. (2003). Audiovisual mirror neurons and action recognition. *Experimental Brain Research*, *153*, 628–636.

Klein, M. (1930/1988). The importance of symbol-formation in the development of the ego. In *Love, guilt and reparation*. London: Virago Press.

Klein, M. (1946/1988). Notes on some schizoid mechanisms. In *Envy and gratitude and other works*. London: Virago Press.

Klein, M. (1958/1988). On the development of mental functioning. In *Envy and gratitude and other works*. London: Virago Press.

Kohler, E., Keysers, C., Umilta, M., Fogassi, L. and Gellese, V. (2002). Hearing sounds, understanding actions: Action representation in mirror neurons. *Science, 297*, 846–848.

Kokkinaki, T. (1998). Emotion and imitation in early infant–parent interaction: A longitudinal and cross-cultural study. Ph.D. thesis, Department of Psychology, University of Edinburgh, Scotland.

Kokkinaki, T. (2003). A longitudinal, naturalistic and cross-cultural study on emotions and imitation in early infant–parent imitative interactions. *British Journal of Developmental Psychology, 21*, 243.

Kokkinaki, T. and Kugiumutzakis, G. (2000). Basic aspects of vocal imitation in infant–parent interaction during the first 6 months. *Journal of Reproductive and Infant Psychology, 18*, 173–188.

Kolb, D. (1985). *Experiential learning: Experience as the source of learning and development*. London: Prentice-Hall.

Kotulak, R. (1993). *Unlocking the mind*. Chicago: Chicago Tribune Series, Chicago Tribune.

Kugiumutzakis, G. (1994). Is early human imitation an emotional phenomenon? In S. Beaten (ed.), *Intersubjective communication and emotion in ontogeny*, Symposium Proceedings, Norwegian Academy of Science and Letters.

Laplanche, J. and Pontalis, J. B. (1988). *The language of psychoanalysis*. London: Karnac.

Latour, B. (1983). Give me a laboratory and I will raise the world. In M. Mulkay (ed.), *Science observed*. Thousand Oaks, CA: Sage.

Lester, B. and Tronick, E. (1994). The effects of prenatal cocaine exposure and child outcome. *Infant Mental Health Journal, 15*, 107–120.

Lester, B., Zachariah Boukydis, C. and Twomey, J. (2000). Maternal substance abuse and child outcome. In C. Zeanah (ed.), *Handbook of infant mental health*. New York: Guilford Press.

Lewkowicz, D. (1989). The role of temporal factors in infant behaviour and development. In I. Levin and D. Zakay (eds), *Time and human cognition: A life-span perspective*. Amsterdam: North-Holland.

Lichtenberg, J. D. (1983). *Psychoanalysis and infant research*. Hillsdale, NJ: Analytic Press.

Lieberman, A. and Zeanah, C. (1999). Contribution of attachment theory to infant–parent psychotherapy and other interventions with infants and young children. In J. Cassidy and P. Shaver (eds), *Handbook of attachment*. New York: Guilford Press.

Lieberman, A., Silverman R. and Pawl, J. (2000). Infant–parent psychotherapy. In C. Zeanah (ed.), *Handbook of infant mental health* (2nd edn). New York: Guilford Press.

Lieberman, A., Van Horn, P., Grandison, C. and Pekarsky, J. (1997). Mental health assessment of infants, toddlers and preschoolers in a service program and a treatment outcome research program. *Infant Mental Health Journal, 18*, 158–170.

Likierman, M. (2001). Melanie Klein: Her work in context. London: Continuum.

Likierman, M. (2003). Post natal depression, the mother's conflict and parent–infant psychotherapy. *Journal of Child Psychotherapy, 29*, 301–315.

Lock, A. (1978). The emergence of language. In A. Lock (ed.), *Action, gesture and symbol*. London: Academic Press.

Lombardi, K. and Lapidos, E. (1990). Therapeutic engagements with children: Integrating infant research and clinical practice. *Psychoanalytic Psychology, 7*, 91–103.

Lopez-Corvo, R. (2003). *The dictionary of the work of W. R. Bion*. London: Karnac.

McDonough, S. (2000). Interaction guidance: An approach for difficult-to-engage families. In C. Zeanah (ed.), *Handbook of infant mental health*. New York: Guilford Press.

Magee, B. (1998). *The story of philosophy*. London: Dorling Kindersley.

Main, M. and Goldwyn, R. (1984a). Predicting rejection of her infant from mother's representation of her own experience: Implications for the abused–abusing intergenerational cycle. *International Journal of Child Abuse and Neglect, 8*, 203–217.

Main, M and Goldwyn, R. (1984b). Adult attachment scoring and classification system. Unpublished manuscript, University of California at Berkeley.

Main, M. and Solomon, J. (1986). Discovery of a new insecure-disorganised/ disoriented attachment pattern. In M. Yogman and B. Brazelton (eds), *Affective development in infancy*. Norwood, NJ: Ablex Press.

Marvin, R., Cooper, G., Hoffmann, K. and Powell, B. (2002). The Circle of Security project: Attachment-based intervention with caregiver–pre-school child dyads. *Attachment and Human Development, 4*, 107–124.

Maslow, A. H. (1970). *Motivation and personality*. New York: Harper and Row.

Mason, J. (1996). *Qualitative researching*. London: Sage.

Maunders, H., Giles, D. and Douglas, H. (in press). Mothers' experiences of their relationships with community health professionals in their children's preschool years. *Community Practitioner*.

Meltzer, D. (1976/1994). Temperature and distance as technical dimensions of interpretation. In A. Hahn (ed.), *Sincerity and other works. Collected papers of Donald Meltzer*. London: Karnac.

Meltzoff, A. and Borton, W. (1979). Intermodal matching by neonates. *Nature, 282*, 403–404.

Meltzoff, A. and Moore, M. K. (1989). Imitation in newborn infants: Exploring the range of gestures imitated and the underlying mechanisms. *Developmental Psychology, 25*, 954–962.

Milford, R., Kleve, L., Lea, J. and Greenwood, R. (2006). A pilot evaluation study of the Solihull Approach. *Community Practitioner, 79*, 358–362.

Miller, L., Rustin, M. and Shuttleworth, J. (1989). *Closely observed infants.* London: Duckworth.

Murray, L. (1991). Intersubjectivity, object relations theory and empirical evidence from mother infant interactions. *International Journal of Infant Mental Health, 12,* 219–232.

Murray, L. and Andrews, L. (2000). *The social baby.* Richmond, Surrey: CP Publishing.

Murray, L. and Trevarthen, C. (1985). Emotion regulation of interactions between two month olds and their mothers. In T. Field and N. Fox (eds), *Social perception in infants.* Norwood, NJ: Ablex.

Music, G. (2004). Review of N. Altman, R. Briggs, J. Frankel, D. Gensler and P. Pantone, *Relational Child Psychotherapy. Journal of Child Psychotherapy, 30,* 367–370.

Nagy, E. and Molnar, P. (1994). Homo imitans or homo provocans? *International Journal of Psychophysiology, 18,* 128.

O'Shaughnessy, E. (1981/1992). A commemorative essay on W. R. Bion's theory on thinking. *Journal of Child Psychotherapy, 7,* 181–189. In E. Bott Spillius (ed.), *Melanie Klein today* (Vol. 2), London: Routledge.

Osofsky, J. (1987). *Handbook of infant development.* New York: Wiley.

Panksepp, J. (2000). The neuro-evolutionary cusp between emotions and cognitions: Implications for understanding consciousness and the emergence of a unified mind science. *Consciousness and Emotion, 1,* 15–54.

Papousek, H. (1967). Experimental studies of appetitional behavior in human newborns and infants. In H. Stevenson, E. Hess and H. Rheingold (eds), *Early behaviour: Comparative and developmental approaches.* New York: Wiley.

Papousek, H. and Papousek, M. (1987). Intuitive parenting: A dialectical counterpart to the infant's integrative competence. In J. Osofsky (ed.), *Handbook of infant development* (2nd edn). New York: Wiley.

Pawl, J. and Lieberman, A. (1997). Infant–parent psychotherapy. In J. Noshpitz (ed.), *Handbook of child and adolescent psychiatry* (Vol. 1). New York: Basic Books.

Perry, B. D. (1995). Childhood trauma, the neurobiology of adaptation and use-dependent development of the brain. *Journal of Infant Mental Health, 16,* 271–291.

Puckering, C., Mills, M., Rogers, J., Cox, A. and Mattsson-Graff, M. (1994). Process and evaluation of a group intervention for mothers with parenting difficulties. *Child Abuse Review, 13,* 299–310.

Reid, M. (1993). Joshua – life after death: The replacement child. *Journal of Child Psychotherapy, 18,* 109–138.

Reid, S. (1990). The importance of beauty in the psychoanalytic experience. *Journal of Child Psychotherapy, 16,* 29–52.

Reid, S. (1997). The development of autistic defences in an infant. *International Journal of Infant Observation, 1,* 51–79.

Ryan, R., Kuhl, J. and Deci, E. (1997). Nature and autonomy: An organizational view of social and neurobiological aspects of self-regulation in behaviour and development. *Development and Psychopathology*, 9, 701–728.

Sackett, G. (1987). Analysis of social interaction data. In J. Osofsky (ed.), *Handbook of infant development*. New York: Wiley.

Scavo, M. C. (2000). Creating supportive approaches for new parents. *The Signal, Newsletter of the World Association for Infant Mental Health*, 8, 1–7.

Schore, A. N. (1994). *Affect regulation and the origin of the self*. Hillsdale, NJ: Lawrence Erlbaum Associates, Inc.

Schore, A. N. (1996). The experience-dependent maturation of a regulatory system in the orbital prefrontal cortex and the origin of developmental psychopathology. *Development and Psychopathology*, 8, 59–87.

Schore, A. N. (2001). Effects of a secure attachment relationship on right brain development, affect regulation and infant mental health. *Journal of Infant Mental Health*, 22, 7–66.

Schore, A. N. (2003). Minds in the making: Attachment, the self-organizing brain, and developmentally-oriented psychoanalytic psychotherapy. In J. Corrigall and H. Wilkinson (eds), *Revolutionary connections: Psychotherapy and neuroscience*. London: Karnac.

Segal, H. (1957/1988). Notes on symbol formation. In E. Bott Spillius (ed.), *Melanie Klein today*. Vol. 1. *Mainly theory*. London: Routledge.

Segal, H. (1979/1988). Postscript 1979: Notes on symbol formation. In E. Bott Spillius (ed.), *Melanie Klein today*. Vol. 1. *Mainly theory*. London: Routledge.

Seifer, R. and Dickstein, S. (2000). Parental mental illness and infant development. In C. Zeanah (ed.), *Handbook of infant mental health* (2nd edn, pp. 145–160). New York: Guilford Press.

Seligman, S. (1994). Applying psychoanalysis in an unconventional context: Adapting infant–parent psychotherapy to a changing population. *Psychoanalytic Study of the Child*, 49, 481–510.

Shonkoff, J. P. and Phillips, D. A. (2000). *From neurons to neighbourhoods: The science of early childhood development*. Washington, DC: National Academy Press.

Shuttleworth, A. (1999). How we have changed. Paper given at ACP 50th Birthday Conference, London.

Shuttleworth, J. (1998a) Theories of mental development. *International Journal of Infant Observation*, 1, 29–50.

Shuttleworth, J. (1998b). An infant observation quoted in Waddell, M., *Inside lives: Psychoanalysis and the development of the personality*. London: Duckworth.

Silverman, D. (2000). *Doing qualitative research*. London: Sage Publications.

Singh, L., Morgan, J. L. and Best, C. (2002). Infants' listening preferences: Baby talk or happy talk? *Infancy*, 3, 365–394.

Skolnick, N. J. and Warshaw, S. C. (1992). *Relational perspectives in psycho-analysis*. Hillsdale, NJ: Analytic Press.

Solomon, J. and George, C. (1999). The measurement of attachment security in infancy and childhood. In J. Cassidy and P. Shaver (eds), *Handbook of attachment*. New York: Guilford Press.

Spangler, G., Fremmer-Bombik, E. and Grossmann, K. (1996). Social and individual determinants of attachment security and disorganisation during the first year. *Infant Mental Health Journal*, *17*, 127–139.

Speltz, M. (1990). The treatment of preschool conduct problems: An integration of behavioral and attachment concepts. In M. Greenberg, D. Cicchetti and M. Cummings (eds), *Attachment in the preschool years: Theory, research and intervention*. Chicago: University of Chicago Press.

Sroufe, L. A. and Waters, E. (1977). Attachment as an organizational construct. *Child Development*, *48*, 1184–1199.

Stern, D. (1985). *The interpersonal world of the infant: A view from psychoanalysis and developmental psychology*. New York: Basic Books.

Stern, D. (1990). Joy and satisfaction in infancy. In R. Glick and S. Bone (eds), *Pleasure beyond the pleasure principle*. New Haven, CT: Yale University Press.

Stern, D. (1998). *Diary of a baby*. New York: Basic Books.

Strauss, A. and Corbin, J. (1998). *Basics of qualitative research*. Thousand Oaks, CA: Sage.

Sullivan, M. and Lewis, M. (2003). Emotional expressions of young infants and children: A practitioner's perspective. *Infants and Young Children*, *16*, 120–143.

Symington, N. (1986). *The analytic experience*. London: Free Association Books.

Trevarthen, C. (1974). Conversations with a two month old. *New Scientist*, May, 1974.

Trevarthen, C. (1980). The foundations of intersubjectivity: Development of interpersonal and co-operative understanding in infants. In D. R. Olson (ed.), *The social foundation of language and thought*. New York: Norton.

Trevarthen, C. (1998). When the holder is beholden, the infant's psyche may be strong. *Infant Observation*, *1*, 105–116.

Trevarthen, C. (1999). Musicality and the intrinsic motive pulse: Evidence from human psychobiology and infant communication. *Rhythms, musical narrative and the origins of human communication. Musicae Scientiae*, Special Issue 1999–2000: 157–213.

Trevarthen, C. (2001). Instrinsic motives for companionship in understanding: Their origin, development and significance for mental health. *International Journal of Infant Mental Health*, *22* (1–2), 95–131.

Trevarthen, C. (2003). Neuroscience and intrinsic psychodynamics: Current knowledge and potential for therapy. In J. Corrigall and H. Wilkinson (eds), *Revolutionary connections: Psychotherapy and neuroscience*. London: Karnac.

Trevarthen, C., Kokkinaki, T. and Flamenghi, G. (1999). What infants' imitations communicate: With mothers, with fathers and with peers. In J. Nadel and G. Butterworth (eds), *Imitation in infancy: Progress and prospects of current research*. Cambridge: Cambridge University Press.

Trevatt, D. (1999). An account of a little boy's attempt to recover from the trauma of abuse. *Journal of Child Psychotherapy, 25*, 267–287.

Tronick, E. Z. (1989). Emotions and emotional communication in infants. *American Psychologist, 44*, 112–126.

Tronick, E. Z. and Cohn, J. (1989). Infant–mother face-to-face interaction: Age and gender differences in co-ordination and occurrence of miscoordination. *Child Development, 60*, 80–92.

Tronick, E. and Gianino, A. (1986). Interactive mismatch and repair: Challenges to the coping infant. *Zero to Three: Bulletin of the National Center Clinical Infant Program, 5*, 1–6.

Tronick, E. Z. and Weinberg, M. K. (1997). Depressed mothers and infants: Failure to form dyadic states of consciousness. In L. Murray and P. J. Cooper (eds), *Postpartum depression and child development*. New York: Guilford Press.

Tronick, E. Z., Cohn, J. and Shea, E. (1986). The transfer of affect between mother and infants. In T. B. Brazelton and M. W. Yoymans (eds), *Affective development in infancy*. Norwood, NJ: Ablex.

Tyhurst, J. (1951). Individual reactions to community disaster. *American Journal of Psychiatry, 10*, 746–769.

Urban, E. (1999). Infant observation, experimental infant research and psychodynamic theory. Paper given at ACP 50th Birthday Conference, London.

van Ijzendoorn, M. (1995). Adult attachment representations, parental responsiveness, and infant attachment: A meta-analysis on the predictive validity of the Adult Attachment Interview. *Psychological Bulletin, 117*, 387–403.

van Ijzendoorn, M. and De Wolff, M. (1997). In search of the absent father: Meta-analysis of infant–father attachment. A rejoinder to our discussants. *Child Development, 68*, 604–609.

Vaughn, B. and Bost, K. (1999). Attachment and temperament. In J. Cassidy and P. Shaver (eds), *Handbook of attachment*. New York: Guilford Press.

Waddell, M. (1998). *Inside lives: Psychoanalysis and the development of the personality*. London: Duckworth.

Wallerstein, R. (1986). *Forty-two lives in treatment: A study of psychoanalysis and psychotherapy*. New York: Guilford Press.

Warner, R., Malloy, D., Schneider, K., Knoth, R. and Wilder, B. (1987). Rhythmic organisation of social interaction and observer ratings of positive affect and involvement. *Journal of Nonverbal Behaviour, 11*, 57–74.

Wells, A. (1997). The beginnings of mind: Psychotherapy of a sexually abused six-year-old girl. In M. Rustin, M. Rhode, A. Dubinsky and H. Dubinsky (eds), *Psychotic states in children*. London: Duckworth.

Whitehead, R. and Douglas, H. (2005). Health visitors' experience of using the Solihull Approach. *Community Practitioner*, *78*, 20–23.

Williams, G. (1997). *Internal landscapes and foreign bodies: Eating disorders and other pathologies*. London: Duckworth.

Williams, G. (1998). Reflections on some particular dynamics of eating disorders. In R. Anderson, and A. Dartington (eds), *Facing it out*. London: Duckworth.

Winkley, L. (1996). *Emotional problems in children and young people*. London: Cassell.

Winnicott, D. (1965). *Maternal processes and the facilitating environment*. New York: International Universities Press.

Wittgenstein, L. (1921/2001). *Tractatus Logico-Philosophicus*. London: Routledge Classics.

Wolf, N. (2003). Bion's infant: How he learns to think his thoughts. *International Journal of Infant Observation*, *6*, 10–24.

Wolff, P. (1965/1974). The development of attention in young infants. In L. Stone, H. Smith and L. Murphy (eds), *The competent infant: Research and commentary*. London: Tavistock.

Zajonc, R. (1985). Emotion and facial efference: A theory reclaimed. *Science*, *228*, 15–22.

Zeanah, C., Boris, N., Heller, S., Hinshaw-Fuselier, S., Larrieu, J., Lewis, M. et al. (1997). Relationship assessment in infant mental health. *Infant Mental Health Journal*, *18*, 182–197.

Index